REDHEAD

ELUNED PHILLIPS

The Reluctant Redhead

Gomer

To
Côr Cymreig De Califfornia;
Côr Merched Llandybïe and Eira Thomas;
Côr Meibion De Cymru.

First Impression – 2007

ISBN 978 1 84323 866 9

A CIP record for this title is available from the British Library.

Printed and bound in Wales at
Gomer Press, Llandysul, Ceredigion, SA44 4JL

Forewarned

To do, or not to do? That was my question. (And I was not aping William Shakespeare – even if he has been my special hero since childhood.) It was this dilemma of biographies, more precisely the 'auto' ones. For some time I have been pressured to write my memoirs, and when I reached my ninetieth birthday in 2004, the pressure became a pain. I had always been convinced that talking, and especially writing, about yourself must be the height of egotism, and believe me, my simple life has been splattered with more than my share of egotists. So the 'To do or not to do' festered.

In the end a simple tinkle of the doorbell solved the crisis. I opened the door, ignoring the politically-correct chain that was meant to stand between me and an intruder. A presentable one at that. He wanted, if I agreed, to write an article about me in a magazine. He added that Ron Davies, Aberaeron, the photographer, had insisted that he should come and talk to me. Now, I have all the time in the world for Ron Davies. We have been friends for years. He is well known throughout Wales and beyond, and his exhibitions are widely acclaimed. Ron has been working from a wheelchair since the motor-cycling accident that befell him when he was sixteen years old, and will tackle shots that most other able-bodied photographers would consider risky. Not once have I heard a note of self-pity. He has my ultimate respect and admiration and I have been honoured to be invited to write mini-poems to complement his amazing photographs. If you ever need a tonic, contact Ron – he is an eternal bubble of humour.

So there was a welcome at the door for David Fielding, the owner and publisher of two magazines, *Carmarthenshire Life* and *Pembrokeshire Life*. He told me candidly that he had never heard of me. I certainly didn't blame him for that. I admitted that I had never heard of him or his magazines either. All to the good. We were now on a level playing field. But when I browsed through the two magazines he had left me, I did blame myself for not having heard of them. They were celebrating their tenth anniversary and I had lost out on years of enjoyable reading. I was hooked and agreed to be interviewed for a page in the October issue of *Carmarthenshire Life*.

Thus, David Fielding presented himself at my home, Glyn-y-Mêl, for a second time, this time clutching his recording machine. I don't particularly dislike recording machines – I'm just a bit wary. I have been caught, more than once, babbling on, non-stop, about my many embarrassing mishaps, only to have to listen to them later on the air, after assurances that they had been strictly off-record. But now I'm ninety plus, who cares anyway; I guess my antique skin no longer blushes.

We settled down to talk. The telephone rang. An American friend, more garrulous than even I can be. Eventually, I went back to apologise. David had disappeared. I found him in the kitchen. He had brewed us a mug of coffee each – delicious – a mixture of latte and a dream. My distrust of his recorder vanished.

Somehow, this gentle Yorkshireman with the soft voice and an inclination to cock his head sideways when asking pertinent questions had such an effect that the words tumbled out. As he said: 'After two-and-a-half hours, we had only reached the Second World War, barely a third of her life.' He had the patience of a saint. We laboured on. The one page became pages in the October, November and December issues. I escaped to Los Angeles before the January issue was born. The final episode was reached in February 2006.

Even after the first article in October, doubtless due to David's charming style of writing, there was a clamour for a full autobiography. And with each subsequent article, the clamour increased – and wore me down. The 'To Do' mentality won.

However, as David Fielding rightly exposed in his interviews, my topsy-turvy nature is such an integral part of me that there would be complications ahead.

Modern life and its boundless technology is not always kind to the old. For years I have had to cope with a computer. Siencyn, my first, and I had many a fight; it was more temperamental than I am. Mice and I have never been comfortable together so I wrote a rather hasty poem to 'The Mouse' in which there were two unforgivable lines:

> I hate mice with a passion
> And this mouse was beyond redemption . . .

Ever since, I have become convinced that these robots are as spiteful as humans.

Siencyn II was slightly more disciplined.

I have a new one now, Tomos ap Siencyn the Second, and it is thanks to it that, these days, I can't help thinking of that wonderful actress, Maureen Lipman. How I sympathised and roared with laughter at her many 'itises'. Now that I have caught an 'itis' myself, tendinitis, I have only a deep, deep sympathy. No one had warned me that this modern disease was contagious. I was clearing my desk to make room for this momentous ninety-years-plus living project, when I came across a dead script, abandoned when I had had my car accidents. Since I have been a Cardi for most of my life, I just had to try to resurrect it. So I went to 'Word' and typed 120 pages – without a single break. I learnt the hard way that new technology doesn't pamper slave workers. As a result, my right wrist is now harnessed and out of bounds for the foreseeable future, and I will have to buy a gadget to talk to Tomos ap Siencyn II if these memoirs are ever to see the light of day. It is a daunting thought. Whilst I am quite happy talking to an audience, I have never found the knack of talking to a soulless machine. Indeed, when I leave a message on an answering machine, I am always surprised that I'm not arrested for spreading a virus!

I am still not convinced that my ninety-years-plus of living will be of interest to people but I will do my best to think along the years. I have never kept a diary and all my friends have given up long ago on my no-filing system. My good friend, the late Les Walters, even bought me endless files and labelled them. Cardigan Jack wanted to fill all the rooms in my bungalow with filing cabinets. Fair play, he is a wonderful researcher and I turn to him with respect when my patience becomes wafer-thin and liable to end up in an inglorious muddle. When Netta, the cleaner, tackles my mantlepiece, I am lost to the world for days.

In finishing this laborious introduction, I would humbly ask one favour. If or, probably, when you get bored with this book, please do not cremate it. I committed a sinful act once. You will have gathered from the title, that red hair and I were reluctant partners. I was the only redhead in the family and stood out like an assaulted thumb. The teasing was unrelenting. Then someone decided to write a book in Welsh entitled *Luned Bengoch* ('Eluned the Redhead'). W.H. Smith in Cardigan gave over a whole window to display copies of this book. My malevolent teasers had a field day. They insisted, very wrongly, that the book was about me. Like Canute, I had to try to stop the tide. I stole posies of daffodils and roses from my mother's garden, sold them around the village for a good cause, and marched boldly in to W.H. Smith and bought all nine copies. I went home and burnt the lot. To this day, my medical records testify that I suffer from an irritable conscience. I have never, ever since burnt a book.

I will do my best to shape these memoirs by talking to Tomos ap Siencyn II. The trivialities will probably come to the fore. There have been doors to close and doors to open. Some keys are lost and will remain so. A red-headed person was not handed out patience at birth to recover memories that should remain lost in the mists of time.

Footprints in Concrete

October 27, 1914. The scene is Glynia, my grandmother's cottage, a mile or so inside the Carmarthenshire boundary of the village of Cenarth. The August bells are still deafening Welsh ears, alerting the world to the 'Great' war with Germany. Patriotic men and women are rising to the call of duty, among them my father. It is the 'War to end all wars'.

I would never see my father: he was killed, fighting for his country. But mine would still be a happy childhood. My grandmother saw to that. She was indomitable, having the spirit of a pioneer, and she, with her eight small children, had once been all set to emigrate and to join my grandfather in America. But he was fatally injured in an accident there before his family had a chance to venture forth. Her name was Marged, but, like most of the neighbours, I called her Mam. She was a female Solomon, dispensing advice and comfort to the needy, whenever and wherever, and was one of the cluster of women who cushioned my early years.

My mother, Mary Ann, I called Mary, or Mari fach (a Welsh endearment), if I wanted a special favour. All those years ago that might have appeared rebellious but it was the result of affection, not disrespect. We were great friends.

My sister, Margaret Elizabeth (or Madge to many) was born two years before me, and I remain convinced that she got more than her fair share of those twin genes of goodness and propriety.

I, Sara Adeline Eluned, was born on October 27. On the very same day in Swansea town, a red-headed baby boy was born. Being male, I guess, was decidedly in his favour. Indeed he would in time become a world icon, and I shall have cause to mention him again.

9

Later we were joined by an orphaned cousin from Swansea, Carbetta Mary (soon called Get), who became my Big Sister, my favourite story-teller and my strict disciplinarian.

For all of which, today, I am truly thankful.

We all snuggled under my gran's extended wings. And how extended they were I would only fully realise later, when, with red-headed rashness, I was rude to a neighbour. Now my gran had an old hen strutting along the yard who looked a bit of a mess: by today's fashionable standards she would have been written off as obese! Everyone called this hen Martha Hael, a silly name for a hen, I thought. Not having started school yet, I didn't know that '*hael*' meant generous. So when I heard a neighbour telling another neighbour that my gran was exactly like Martha Hael, and both having a good laugh about it, my flaming hair lit up further. However, when they explained to me that they were actually complimenting my adored gran, I started taking an interest in old Martha Hael and found what a dear old motherly soul she was, gathering anybody in need under her wings. She would cuddle young ducklings stranded from their mother; kittens on the yard would snuggle under her, and even the old family spaniel would have a glint in his pleading eyes when allowed to almost ruffle her feathers. Martha Hael and my grandmother were definitely two of a kind. Yes, thanks to her, childhood was fun.

Later we crossed the bridge at Cenarth to Cardiganshire and I became a Cardi for the rest of my life. First at Glanawmor, a lovely detached house, guarded each side by two ancient oak trees, six acres of greenery and the friendly stream of Awmor as it snaked its way into the river Teifi.

Today, and alone, I am in our retirement bungalow, Glyn-y-Mêl, built across the road from Glanawmor when we finally accepted that old age was speeding towards us with the studied concentration of a racing driver.

In the name of progress, my old home is now surrounded by buildings. In our orchard there are six houses. The cottage down the garden has become a bungalow. The pigsty and the stable are almost all the residences of incomers from the other side of Offa's Dyke. Sometime ago, when I left for one of my visits to America, a property developer started laying the foundation of another building, sited almost on top of the stream, right beside the busy Carmarthen to Cardigan road. When I came back, a huge building had mushroomed – it could have been a jail or a church, for all I knew. Now three more have followed. Who knows, it may soon become a community in its own right. My village, like so many in Wales, is galloping to become a centre of tourism.

It is difficult, at times, to capture and preserve the old magic.

For many years now, I have, thanks to repeated invitations, given talks at home and abroad, sometimes in Welsh, sometimes in English and often in both languages. They are chatty talks, not posh, expensive after-dinner affairs, although I must confess that I'm always well fed beforehand! Invariably I am asked at post-mortem discussions:'Have you written them down?' I never have. Didn't think they were that important. So the recording of these reminscences, their preserving, if you like, is trial-and-error time. And I am at the mercy of my memory.

One of my most frequently requested talks is entitled 'Some footprints in concrete'. This generally generates blank stares from my audience and I have to hasten to explain. As I will now!

When we decided to build our retirement bungalow, we were lucky enough to find a prominent builder living not far away. He was an Italian ex-prisoner of war, whose family had been builders for generations, and he was married to a lovely Welsh valley girl. His name was Rago and he, with his son Tanino, unlike some builders, was prepared to finish our bungalow and not move on to other jobs before construction was complete. Excellent. In this modern world, I, too, have had to become an 'instant' living being. I boldly designed my own bungalow with its two open fireplaces (with hindsight, an extravagant, wishful dream, since I have never found time for cosy sittings). Rago, when he saw my sketch plan, pointed out that I would also need a door to go in! Bless him. I now have three. My only contention with him was that he was a perfectionist. I wanted to peep and find out what he was doing with my designs. He was adamant, however, that I would have to wait until he had perfected everything. To one with my colouring, such an injunction was decidedly the proverbial red rag to a bull!

But, one day, I happened to be passing when he was laying the floor of the garage. At that very moment, I saw him deliberately putting his heavy working boot in the wet concrete. Perfection? What perfection? I went straight for the jugular and accused him of sheer vandalism. He in turn let rip a mouthful of long, Italian words. At any other time I would have found them sweetly musical to the ear. But not now. My red hair, in fiery flames, was twirling a tango. I demanded an explanation that I could understand.

He obliged. None of his ancestors would ever leave a building they had created without fixing their stamp on it, and once the mark was set in concrete, it could never be deleted. I stole the title unashamedly there and then: 'Footprints in concrete'. As in my talks, therefore, I will write about all the people who have left an indelible mark on my life.

There are no prizes for forecasting who will take centre stage in my next chapter.

My Grandmother

I would like to think that I inherited some of my grandmother's genes. I was certainly denied, however, her physical stature. Though I may at one time have boasted five feet three inches, 'Mam' was a six-footer at least, her back as straight and solid as an old-fashioned telegraph pole. Fearless, too. She would travel alone in a trap and pony over the wild moors from Newcastle Emlyn to Carmarthen Market, sometimes returning, very late at night, with only her leaden-top walking stick to protect her from would-be highwaymen.

But, all my life, I have treasured what she did pass on to me. She inspired my love of literature when I was very young. And mere thanks could never recompense the thrill of that.

Gran was brought up at Aberdwylan Farm on the banks of the river Cych, a tributary of the River Teifi. When I was a child, she would take me to nearby Cwmcych, where, according to the *Mabinogi*, Pwyll Pendefig Dyfed used to bring his hunting dogs. Oh, the joy! I could see the dogs, white bodies and red ears (or maybe it was the other way round) streaking through the trees. Years later, I found that my gran's story didn't really match those medieval tales, but it had instilled in me a great love of Welsh literature.

Even more thrilling than the *Mabinogi* was the story she told of her eight brothers, building a boat in their yard at Aberdwylan, launching it on the Cych, then on to the Teifi, before finally reaching the port at Cardigan. Thus, I guess, the sense of adventure seeped into my veins. If only one could buy time to recapture the wonders of the past.

All my family were millers, carpenters and millwrights and can be traced back as far as 1101. The only one I can vaguely

13

remember, however, is my mother's cousin. He lived in Dwylan House, which had been built by my family, as had Mill Lodge, both in the village of Cenarth. Unfortunately in those days, such houses had to be built on leased lands to be confiscated at will by unethical landlords. This, and the absolute pressure of voting for pot-bellied squires, resulted in my grandfather and three of my grandmother's brothers emigrating to find freedom of mind in America. My mother's cousin was just plain Henry Jones. His 17th-century forerunner, however, was Sir Henry Jones. With justification, or for convenience, the title was mislaid in a world of dog eats dog.

There was another bonus, a big one as it turned out, in being the grandchild of my mercurial grandmother. She was a midwife to the gypsies – each of them of true Romany stock in those days. There was an enormous lay-by outside Cenarth village on the Carmarthenshire side, called Banc y Shiftwn ('The Gypsy Embankment'). Gypsy families would travel a long way to be back at this embankment whenever a birth was imminent in order to secure the services of my gran. On such occasions I used to clutch at my gran's skirt and follow her into all the caravans. And what a welcome I would get! They oozed with magical treasures. I knew all the Romany families – the Lovells, the Boswells, the John Evanses, the Duttons et al.

Maybe little girls with red hair are more inquisitive than their brown-locked counterparts, but I never seem to remember my brunette sister being part of this intriguing scene. They were mostly law-abiding, friendly travellers. I only heard of one instance when maybe they bent the law a little. There was a farmer whose fields were near the encampment. He was known as a miser and was forever spying in case the gypsy horses encroached on one blade of grass from his field. Fair play, I suppose the gypsy men had to retaliate. In the early hours of one morning, they sent in their horses after tying some heavy material around the hooves to disguise their footmarks. The horses must have thought they had reached paradise. They happily grazed down to the quick. John Parcybras stamped and raved when he found out but the neighbours thought he had been justly reprehended.

Life can be abruptly inconsiderate, especially when you're young. It was a sad night when I severed my connection with my gypsy friends. It had been a wonderful festive occasion. The Lovell clan had been gloriously generous. My midwife grandmother had helped to deliver a son and the celebrations were magic. Gran was elevated to the status of a queen and I wasn't going to miss out on feeling royal, too. The gypsy men had gathered stray branches from the wood nearby and we sat around a crackling bonfire. There was dancing and singing but my eyes kept on straying to a kind of clay football sitting in the middle of the hot flames. I wanted to ask my gran about it but so many Romanies wanted to talk to her that I didn't have a chance. Then it was time to eat. They rolled out the football from the fire and the father of the newborn cracked it open. Inside was a roasted hedgehog! They only saw my heels as I ran all the way home. After all, I had my own little hedgehog in the garden and I would put out a saucer of milk for it night and morning. Thus ended those idyllic gypsy incidents. In the morning I had to face a very stern grandmother. Not only had I been discourteous to her Romany friends, but I had lost the tastiest meal I could ever have wished for. As a kind of apology, I added a little cream to my hedgehog's milk that night.

I don't think my grandmother would have understood the word 'apartheid'. She was class-less and treated high and low as human beings. I remember once Lord Cawdor pulling up at her cottage in a rare expensive car, wanting to speak to her. She had just spotted old Daniel Cwmllydrew walking very unsteadily along the road. He had drunk himself into being a homeless tramp. Gran waved her hand to the rich lord to acknowledge he was waiting for her, and for the next half-hour tried, through advice and admonition, to rescue old, drunken Daniel from his destructive self.

She actually had a regular line of tramps calling with her for food and counsel. When she died, my mother adpoted them, and when she died, they automatically bequeathed themselves to me. When we had moved to Glanawmor, they used to call, one by one, roughly about once a month. We would give them supper, then send them to the next farm, Alltybwla, to sleep in the outhouses, and then back to us for breakfast. They were a different breed from the tinkers of today. Most had been forced to take to the road when problems became unsolvable – maybe through drink, marital turmoil, debts or even because they had been slighted in love.

We thought of the regulars as friends more or less, and attached names to them in our own minds. There was Wil Roses, for example. His name was easy. He had been a gardener at Dinefwr Castle, Llandeilo. His marital problems became too much, so he gathered all his beloved gardening tools into a perambulator, and took to the road. We had a rose garden at the time and the flowers needed pruning. He volunteered and each monthly visit it would be his pride and joy to keep the blooms in order. I wasn't allowed to go near them. I think he missed his obvious vocation.

Dic Polly got his name because there was a lady in nearby Newcastle Emlyn, called Polly, and our tall tramp and her husband were lookalikes. He had a Welsh signature tune, '*Dacw nghariad i lawr yn y berllan*' ('There is my loved one down in the orchard'), to signal each visit, and he was the first man I ever saw wearing rows of colourful beads around his neck. He was definitely my first hippy.

I will have to leave the others, but only after telling you about Paddy – a small, one-armed man, who made up for any defects by being very Irish. Lost his arm, I believe, in a drunken brawl. He was slightly inebriated each time be came by, but was never too drunk to sing. His visits were always a kind of world drama. First he would offer his one hand for a handshake – and the one shake was repeated six times. He would then have his supper or breakfast, depending on the time. After his meal, the same performance of six handshakes was repeated. I have never found out whether this was a typical Irish-Celtic ritual or merely Paddy's own 'Thank you'. Before leaving each time, he would sing two or three old Irish songs in a gloriously melodic tenor voice. I admit to feeling rather cheated when the 1948 Welfare Act rounded such free spirits off the road and herded them into fortresses of bricks and mortar.

I did miss those old characters. I had grown up with them since childhood and had helped them along as best I could. I simply had to, since I took great store of my grandmother's advice when things needed to be done: 'Go for it girl. Give it your best shot'. My lifelong difficulty has been, however, that my best shots always seem to ricochet and become embarrassments. At my age now, I've come to accept this as an inherent weakness. But when you're young, a faux pas is not easy to live down. I remember once being home from school when there was a knock at the door. I ran to answer it to save my tired mother. A gentleman stood there and I heard the word 'tea'. My mother was used to feeding the homeless so I rushed to the kitchen to put the kettle on. Then I went to ask whether he took sugar and milk in his tea. When he was slow in answering, I looked properly at the man. I gawked. He was the best dressed man I had ever seen – far more classy than the preachers who came to preach at my Bryn Seion chapel. It turned out that he was a well-known tea merchant from Llanrhystud, Ceredigion. He and my mother were good friends and she had for years been ordering tea in bulk from him. When he was invited in to have proper tea with us, with a sly wink he told me that he did take sugar in his tea. It all ended with unrelenting teasing and a rollicking laugh at my expense.

Another of my grandmother's legacies to me was the art of listening. It took me years to work out how this simple art worked. But the eternally-open door at my grandmother's cottage and afterwards at Glanawmor and Glyn-y-Mêl helped me to appreciate it, such was the steady stream of callers.

One caller in particular intrigued me. My mother had a friend Katie, married to Philip John James, living at Cilfod Farm, not far away. Katie was a lovely lady but there would be torrid times when she would appear at my gran's place. The moment she was inside the house, the words would tumble out in a rush also. Sometimes she would stay for hours, and eat with us. I was too young to understand any of it. Katie would talk but my grandmother would listen silently, with only an occasional word of comfort. Often, many, many hours later, Katie would jump up suddenly and tell my gran, '*Jiawl* ['Damn'], Marged, I wouldn't go back at all to him but the cows need milking.' Another time it would be '*Jiawl*, Marged, I wouldn't go back at all to him but I have bread in the oven.' Thus Katie would convince herself of a vital reason for always returning to her husband. Philip John was not a bad man. There were times when he confessed that 'John Barley' would seize control of him and he would return home to set saucepans, frying pans, or any other available missiles, flying, and whose target unfortunately would be his wife. Katie, having unloaded her frustrations on a silent listener, would, with renewed strength, take up her normal life again.

I grew old enough to understand. I tried to emulate my grandmother's open door and silent listening. I can only hope that a few of her virtuous genes have somehow stuck to, what somebody, justifiably called, my topsy-turvy life.

Childhood

I spent the first four years of my life in the shadow of the First World War, possibly subject to, but never aware of, its deprivations. I was the baby of the family, after all, and was probably wrapped in cotton wool. It was, thus, a happy childhood.

I hardly remember any bought toys. That was no worry. I was a country girl and enjoyed the company of wildlife. I had a pet hedgehog. I even brought home once, wrapped in my pinafore, a bunch of baby rabbits left motherless by a greedy trapper. I developed a great affinity for climbing trees. Somehow, red hair or not, I have never raged when the occasional know-all insists that we have evolved from monkeys. Later there was nut and blackberry gathering and eventually I was let into the secret world of trout tickling by my playmate, Willie Cilfod, son of the aforementioned Katie. And when it came to pony-riding, that proved my entrance to a seventh heaven.

I did venture once on a shopping expedition, however. It was my fifth or sixth birthday. I had been given some money and taken on a rare trip to Carmarthen. I was all eyes and almost immediately they fell on a banjo in a shop window. I don't know whether I really knew what it was, but it became my birthday present. I never could explain why that instrument was so important to me. Maybe it was the stories my gran used to tell me about my grandfather. He was a rather impressive fiddler – the instrumental not the criminal kind! I often wished that I had known him. But my wishful thoughts, like footprints in the sand, have a way of disappearing. I never played my banjo. I never found a tutor. After all, no one in the village had ever even touched a banjo. So it sulked in the attic – until I bade it a rather nostalgic farewell when it became time to move across the road to a smaller residence.

As children, we were never bored. We entertained visitors with improvised skits. My sister and I would become preachers. Standing on the kitchen table, I would bellow out my sermons. Though Madge had the better brain, I am convinced that my sermons were better because mine made for much more laughter! But when it came to praying, she would beat me hands down. I had to go under the table to deliver: I could not pray in public – and I still can't. Another of my childhood dreams was thus destroyed: I would never become a preacher. My sister, though, blossomed. Although taking up science as a career, she was a licensed lay preacher for many years in Staffordshire.

Another way of entertaining visitors was auctioneering. I was a dab hand at selling all my mother's willow pattern china collection, especially the pieces on the Welsh dresser in the cottage down the garden. Auctioneering was another career I fancied when very young. But that was a non-starter, too. My mother put a firm foot down. It wasn't, apparently, lady-like. Such discrimination seems to have dogged me all my life. A cousin of ours, with only £20 in his pocket, decided on buying and selling property in London, and is now a millionaire, possibly a billionaire. He is male, of course.

My third choice of career was that of a chemist. I had no luck there either: a firm family 'No' again. To an ambitious six-year-old, their subsequent reasoning seemed a bit below the belt. They claimed that because I was always scribbling poetry (and consequently having my head in the clouds), I would cause a scandal by poisoning a customer! I did, however, have another sudden but serious try a few years later when I was at the grammar school. I discovered then that I would have to study Latin, which I had carelessly dropped, so the kind headmaster allowed Jack Bethania (who wanted to be a doctor) and me to take up Latin again and pass it in one term. Jack did become a doctor (a chest consultant no less) but I was only brilliant in scansion, probably because I really did enjoy writing poetry.

But even writing poetry brought unusual trouble sometimes. I was seven years old and had written a poem,which someone saw and sent to a local paper. Tom Morgan, Carreg Lwyd, read it and told my mother, 'Never. She could never have written it.' The old adage 'Gwyn y gwêl y frân ei chyw' ('The black crow sees her offspring as white') held true as both my accuser and I were ordered into the house. My mother gave me pen and paper and told me to sit at the table. She then ordered the man to give me a subject for a poem. He was a forester in charge of Lord Cawdor's woods in the area so, naturally, he suggested 'The tree feller'. Unfortunately he had cut down my favourite climbing tree and I did feel sore – so I wrote my poem about him as a murderer!

Life at times can be so unfair. My poem won my critic over, but I got a most severe scolding for the 'murderer' theme. He and my mother were good friends and she would get the waste branches that he trimmed for firewood. Oddly enough, many years later, I would again be accused of not writing my own poems. I offered my detractors my mother's solution: I would write one under supervision. The offer was not taken up. Sadly, I lost the respect I had for those I had always admired. I have never found out whether it's redheads they don't like in Wales – or merely women who have the audacity to write poetry.

I was accused, too, of publishing all too rarely. It may be lack of ambition or lack of confidence, but I have never written or published anything unless I have been asked or commissioned to do so. When I am asked, I just try to do my best. When that lovely and talented writer Jennie Eirian took over the editing off the Welsh weekly Y Faner, she wrote and asked me if I would write an article for the first edition. I did, and kept on writing a few more for her. I remember then receiving a severe grilling from D. Tecwyn Lloyd for not submitting a poem to Taliesin, the Welsh cultural journal. When, however, he invited me to contribute, I was very willing to oblige, so thinking he needed to fill space, I sent him a rather lengthy one. That didn't please either, so I sent a shorter one. I have never found out why men seem to treat women writers differently. A bit late now, I suppose, to find out.

All this is in stark contrast to America where, in recent years, I have found doing creative work is like a breath of fresh air. If you have any ability, it is appreciated, whether you are male, female, young or old, rich or poor. If occasionally luck comes my way, I am cheerfully thankful.

Looking back, there are many laughs. I missed out on fame and a place in the *Guinness Book of Records* when I was very young. I was on the stage in my village concert dressed in a silk, ivory frock, trimmed with embroidered pears, one that almost fitted a Barbie doll later. I was so nervous in front of such a large audience that I rolled my dress right up to my chin. It seems I had a stunning reception. Definitely the first stripper in Cenarth! I was even paid for it. As I came off the stage, a lovely lady, Mrs Maggie Thomas, Berllan, squeezed a threepenny bit into my hand. I was only two-and-a-half years of age or I might have thought of it as a serious profession. I took part in a lot of concerts after, fully clothed, but still got a threepenny piece each time. It was a lot of money in those war days. She was a lovely lady, one of a whole family who had moved to a farm outside Cenarth from Cefneithin. At that time, I had never heard of Cefneithin and thought it must be another country.

I was generally a quick learner when quite young, especially when it came to picking up poems and songs. But this didn't always work in my favour. Katie Cilfod always liked horticultural shows and my mother would often go with her. Haverfordwest Show was always a must, and if there was a trip of any kind, I tagged along. I muddled along cheerfully at the show but the greatest excitement was reserved for the return journey. My mother had a cousin, a captain on the Irish ferry, at Fishguard, so we had to call to say 'Hello'. Going on a ship was almost better than going into a gypsy caravan.

My mother and Katie were busily talking to the captain so I wandered off. One of the crew kindly took me in hand and down to the galley where the cook gave me all sorts of titbits, and asked me to sing a song. Which I did. I was, after all, used to doing this when we had visitors at home. The sailors were a friendly lot and lifted me on to the table and taught me two songs. The tunes were easy and I soon picked up the words. I was sorry when it was time to leave. My mother thanked everyone for looking after me. I was keeping my two songs secret so that I could surprise my mother when we had visitors calling.

The first visitor the following day was our minister. I always had to sing or recite for him. This time there was no need to ask twice. I sang my two new songs with glee. I was rather disgusted with my mother who tried to stop me from singing the second one. When I finished, I didn't get the smile of pride I generally got. In fact it was a dark frown of disapproval as my mother almost begged the minister to remember that I was only a child. The child, in fact, had been singing two very bawdy sea shanties to a man of the cloth. A long time afterwards, when I realised the extent of my crime, I rather fancy that the reverend gentleman had really enjoyed hearing some very unusual ungodly words. In fact, I got two gentle pats on my head and an almost wicked smile when he left.

My sister and I often performed together in concerts: we recited, wrote our own verses, sang them and accompanied one another. We even scripted and acted sketches. And, of course, we both competed at eisteddfodau. Indeed, it was during preparation for these cultural festivals that my mother and I didn't always quite see eye to eye. I guess I might have had an easier time of it if I had been a respectable twelfth-hour person. Unfortunately I was a thirteenth-hour-plus creator – and there were deadlines and deadlines. Somehow the grey cells didn't really respond until after midnight. And the habit stuck; I am still a midnight owl.

School Days

There was no school in Cenarth during my schooldays. In fact I am very proud that a plot of our land eventually became the entrance to a new school, where pupils from a wide area now congregate.

I must have been a strong and sturdy child, for I started school when I was four years old, even though I had well over two miles to walk. It was then a fairly new building, almost at the bottom end of the village of Abercych. But my sister, who had already started school before me, and I had Olympic minders guarding us – the Smithy boys, Fred, Emlyn and Wil, all tempered at their father's anvil. We were as favoured as any royal offspring.

I don't remember wearing clogs, but I probably did, like most of the other children. I do remember the old brogues wearing out at a rapid speed, when we got the boys to cut sticks from the hedges so that we could play our own improvised hockey. The Cenarth crowd hardly ever went on the main road, but cut across the Penlan woods before crossing a rather do-it-yourself bridge over the Cych at Penrhyn, thus avoiding walking all the way down the village. In summer we would paddle in the warm, clear water of the river and in the hard winters of that time, we would have long stretches of ice on the fields, as good as any ice-rinks I have since seen on my travels. I suppose our healthy cheeks, rosy from the exercise, saved us from the penalties for being late.

There were no hot school-dinners. No burgers – just plain, wholesome, old-fashioned sandwiches. There was an open fireplace in the classroom, and when it was bitterly cold, we would place our bottles of tea to warm by the fire and dream of the *cawl* ('broth') that would be awaiting us after we returned home.

I loved going to school but I must confess that my first day's behaviour didn't augur too well. Naturally a four-year-old would be expected to settle down and have fun with the other youngsters playing with a collection of toys. I was adamant, however: no toys! I decided I wanted to be with the older children in Standard One. Unreasonably, I won. Years after, I often wondered if, seeing my red hair, they had reckoned it was easier to give in rather than suffer a silly kid with tantrums.

'Miss', my first teacher, was a lovely lady. I don't think she was ever trained to teach, but she had a common-sense way with us monsters that would be a blessing for any modern headteacher. I found out later that she did have a name after the 'Miss': Lizzie Ann Jones. I adored her, especially when I was chosen to be in the action songs she would teach us to sing at local concerts. We even performed once at the Pavilion, Cardigan. We were singing 'Who'll buy my caller herring' (Irish, I think) and I spent the previous sleepless night worrying that the fish would slip out of my hand. All went well, thankfully, but I kept my distance from herring for a long, long time afterwards.

When I moved up, I had two new teachers, sisters as it happens. They were always known as Miss Griffiths *Fowr* ('Big') and Miss Griffiths *Fach* ('small'). No grudges to report there and thankfully none from them, either.

Then there was *Mishtir* ('Master'). He was a Mr Evans from somewhere but we all called him 'Sir'. I never heard him speaking Welsh. I did hear Mrs Evans do so, however, and she was a gentle, generous lady, offering us fallen apples when we passed her house. We had a lesson once or twice a week in Welsh, but always sang English songs like 'Drink to me only with thine eyes' or 'I shot an arrow' or some old community songs of the time, I guess. They had a daughter, Rosalind. She was older than I and she, too, had red hair – but I never heard the boys shouting nicknames at her. They wouldn't have dared, presumably, because she was her father's daughter. But I really liked Mishtir. I think I must have been a bit of a favourite, too, because as I got older I was the one he picked to fetch his weekly ration of tobacco from the Post Office and stores at Penrhiw, a long walk away at the other end of the village. How I enjoyed delivering his comfort packet! I was even allowed into the headmaster's sanctum. There, stood a huge globe of the whole world, and I would be allowed to stay and my imagination would run riot as I traced all the different countries with their tongue-twisting names. What a joy! My family would probably disapprove of childhood fascination with that big, wide world, because I am convinced that it was partly the cause of those itchy feet of mine, that even now are reluctant to keep still.

The old school at Abercych is now closed. Sadly, I was there to televise its demise. The village roles have been reversed and children no longer walk miles to school but are bused to the new school at Cenarth.

Before I leave my primary school behind, I should confess that I nearly missed out on going there at all after my first week at Abercych – on going to any school, actually. The boys, and even some of the girls, were calling me all sorts of nicknames – the worst one, the one that made me really apoplectic, was the Welsh one, *cochen*. It only means 'redhead' but to me as a child it sounded like the ranting of a diabolic dinosaur from that sinful place, Sodom, that Dafi Cefen (a minister who occasionally preached at my chapel) always warned us about.

Big-headed, having started school, I decided I would get rid of my wrongly coloured hair. I would have black hair just like my mother. I knew exactly how to do it. And a very old friend of mine, Dafi Jams, Bwlchmelyn, would help. He was a road worker in charge of a length of road in front of my grandmother's cottage. Whenever I had been up to mischief, I used to hide behind him until he had appeased my mother and I would escape with a far less severe scolding. When it was road-tarring time, they would have large casks of coal tar ready on the road. On this particular Saturday, it was time to tar old Dafi's stretch of road. He had taken off the lid of the cask and had gone to sit under a tree further down to enjoy his can of tea. I found an old box and dragged it across the road. I stood on it and plunged my head into the cask, a sure way of getting black hair, thought I. Luckily for me, old Dafi had heard me dragging the box over the stones. He looked and saw only my legs. He said afterwards that he had never moved so quickly in all his life. He was just in time to prevent me choking. My mother, like the others, had such a fright that she forgot to scold me. Instead, they had to shave my head. I was delighted to wear a cap to school, that is until old Dafi told me that when my hair grew again, it would probably be a brighter red colour.

Just my luck. It was, of course, a case of being born too soon. These days I could have tinted my hair any fashionable colour I wished and everyone would have applauded. I am, possibly, the only woman in the world who really looked forward to having grey hair.

Anyway, red hair or not, I passed my Eleven Plus (or was it Ten Plus?) into the Grammar School at Cardigan, and there, I settled down. It was almost a non-embarrassing time since I don't remember any real mishaps. I'm convinced that this was because we had the admirable Dr Rees as headmaster. He had this revered, almost biblical look that automatically aborted misbehaviour. He oozed a respect that I can still feel today.

The only near-daring revolt we ever managed during his reign was on one St David's Day. Our Mathematics teacher was a Dr Parker, a brilliant scholar and a truly pleasant gentleman – but English to the core. We decided in class that we would make a stand for our Welshness. We knew we were not strong enough to battle it out with words – he would flatten even a genius amongst us. So, on March 1, knowing we had two long afternoon lessons of maths, we all, as arranged, displayed our national emblems on our breasts. Not the delicate daffodils but some showpiece leeks. The ones with the biggest, and the strongest smelling specimens, would position themselves for that day in the front seats. Talk about a school riot! The good doctor spent half the lesson in a growling roar, ordering the front-seat smellers to the back of the class! But since there wasn't a single spoilsport in class that day, this did not ease matters. When, by way of apology, we offered the victim some smelling salts, an American cyclone would have left us less battered. Finally he ordered us to solve some non-terrestrial calculations before we left the school premises. Sadly we all had to agree that our Saint David did not come to our rescue.

I spent my final year under the new headmaster, a Mr Thomas Evans. Like his predecessor, but maybe a little more approachable, he was a decided leader for us all. He was the one who let me and Jack Bethania (his father was minister of Bethania Baptist chapel) sit Latin in one term. He had the patience of Job but I was a little embarrassed at times when he would suddenly shout 'come down to earth Eluned'. It was this poetic wandering again as I really was only interested in the rhythms and metres of that almost dead language.

Another Thomas Evans, of Corona drinks fame, was a well-known name in our district and made finding a nickname for our new principal a straightforward task: he would be 'Twm Pop'! Of course, we had too much respect to let him know what we all called him. He was a genuinely great headmaster and came to take an interest in all his past pupils. Indeed, even years later, he used to call at my home. He called once when my sister was home from Staffordshire. She, of course had been Dr Rees's pupil and I wanted her to meet my nice Mr Evans, and with my customary speak-before-you-think hat on, I yelled to her 'Come here Madge. I want to introduce you to Twm Pop.' Oops!

I needn't have worried. He just laughed and said that he had always known what we had called him. All the same I did get a telling off from my sister for what she called my 'runaway' tongue. She, lucky thing, managed to go through life without the embarrassment of a single such faux pas. Amazing!

Having finally abandoned my obsession with being a chemist, I was starting to think 'What next?' When I was younger, the teacher's calling was sacrosanct; that was the profession all mothers prayed that their daughters would enter. I, however, knew instinctively that with my red-headed temperament, I would not survive. What is more, I already had another lead and I would put my case at a family conference.

Cenarth, in those far-off days, had a Women's Institute society. I became a member when I was barely twelve years old thanks to Mrs Evans, an influential lady in the village who had taken me under her wing. She, too, had red hair and had lived for years in India so I was a fascinated follower.

Anyway, a competition was held inviting the members to write a play – in English, of course. Mrs Evans ordered me to send in an entry. Since I would have gone to the moon if she'd asked me, that evening I raided the bookshelves at home and found a particularly heavy biblical tome by Josephus. Urged on by his example, I wrote my masterpiece: 'The Fall of Jerusalem'. And in it went. (Today, given some of our age's literary oddities, it may well have been hailed as the work of a budding genius!) The subsequent adjudication, I sincerely believe, changed my life. The adjudicator was the celebrated Simon B. Jones, one of the Cilie dynasty of poets – not that that meant much to me at the time. Years later, however, I came to know, admire and respect the whole family – one of the jewels of Welsh culture. Simon must have had the kindest heart in creation. His verdict: 'In reading "The Fall of Jerusalem" I found touches of the bard, William Shakespeare.' I was too young (or stupid) to recognize the kindly let-down. From that time on, I was destined to be a writer.

I'll tell you later where such optimistic egotism led me. But first let me tell you about those people of my own square mile.

My Chapel

Bryn Seion. It has been there for me for almost the whole of my life. I don't quite remember but I guess I trotted along there with my big sister Get, and my sister Madge, even before I started school at four years of age. It stands in a lovely countrified spot, perched on a bank, like a stout guardian angel. I find a tranquil welcome each time I walk up the slope, even now when our services are generally held in the vestry as we lose our members, one by one, without replacement. It is a peace that is now almost as extinct as the dinosaurs.

It is a solidly built chapel and I wistfully hope that maybe some of my ancestors living in nearby Aberdwylan had lent a hand in its construction. Along the years I have been to many countries and seen and entered very many chapels, churches, temples, cathedrals, mosques even, some with stunning paintings, some with sculptures, some dripping with gold decorations, but never has my heart jumped with such joy as when I step inside my simple little Bryn Seion. And believe me it deserves homage, if only as the birthplace of the two brothers, Herber and Justin Evans, both acclaimed bilingual preachers far beyond the confines of Wales. Herber Evans left a legacy of powerful hymns sung today with the vigour of his vision. I have listened to a few of the greats preaching in my little chapel. And let me not forget how blessed we are in our present minister, Wynford Thomas, Master of Theology, and a son of that friendly town of Llandovery. What an abundant talent: a powerful preacher, a communicator of humour, a captivating singer, and an every-Sunday organist at our little chapel! May he long reign over us.

I have fond memories of the chapel of my childhood. I used

to sit staring in pride and awe at the sculptured *sedd fawr* ('great pew') and pulpit, hand carved by a blind man. John Miles, Werngoy, was a distant relative so I felt I was entitled to acknowledge him with reverence and joy.

There was another blind person around when I was quite young, whom I remember with fondness. He had been our chapel minister but I think he was retired when I knew him. He used to call at my home and, being blind, he would walk arm in arm with me along the lanes. I think he was the first poet I ever met, because he was called Gwallter Ddu (Black Walter)) by everyone. His proper name I found later was the Rev. D.D. Walters. My uncles told me in later years that he was a very well-known scholar and powerful preacher whose sermons used to stir the miners in the Welsh valleys. He used to listen to and remark on my fledgling poems at the time. I have always been shy of reciting my poems to people but because he was blind, I suppose, I was more forthcoming and always looked forward to our meetings. And it wasn't a one-way meeting of minds, either. He would tell me his thoughts. I couldn't understand half of what he was telling me but he seemed to enjoy it, too. His chief interest seemed to be a man called Karl Marx and his importance to people. In my childish ignorance, I soon put Karl Marx on a par with Father Christmas! Years later I understood his political significance but I never recaptured the excitement that inspired me when listening to my kind-hearted blind friend, Gwallter Ddu, telling me about him.

When we were young, we had a long period without a minister and I am certain that my sister and I benefited from this enormously in later life, especially when it came to public speaking. It was a time when we were trained to take part in discussions, debates and various activities by two deacons, Ben Jones and Richard Rees. Two saints, the equals of Saint David – in fact, much more friendly and accessible, since they were always there to answer my childish questions. They were two very different characters: Ben Jones, slow, careful of thought and stride, knew his Bible inside out; Richard Rees, quick, unexpected and exciting like a shooting star, with a penchant for motorcycles and an aptitude for teaching us the rudiments of tonic sol-fa. The first we nicknamed 'Solomon Slow', the second 'Thunder Clap'.

I was generally on my best behaviour in chapel. Maybe I took to heart the fire-and-brimstone-for-our-sins bellowed at us by the old dramatic preachers. Indeed I can only honestly remember being reprehended once for not behaving solemnly in a service. It was a very, very cold day. All the lamps had been lit to warm up the building. There were icicles on the ceiling. We had a visiting preacher, the Rev. Evans from Saron, Llangeler. He was well into a prayer and I should have had my eyes tightly shut, but I had persuaded myself that peeping with one eye wasn't such a terminal sin. The icicles were thawing and I was just in time to see a huge blob of cold water descending on the unprotected bald head of the preacher still in the throes of a deep prayer. I shouted clearly, 'Look out.' I had a whole congregation of disapproving eyes focused on me. I tried to explain to my big sister, but she shut me up and made me apologise to Mr Evans, I explained to him that I was afraid the shock of the cold water could have given him a heart attack. He thanked me for being such a thoughtful little girl but said that he only listened to God's voice when praying. I understood then why, after I warned him, he just went on praying with his eyes still tightly shut.

One of my annual highlights as a child was the *Cymanfa Ganu*, the Hymn-singing Festival. This was held at our main chapel, Ebenezer, Newcastle Emlyn and a trip there was always a thickly-underlined calendar date. From about the age of seven onwards, it was my duty to recite a psalm at one of the sessions. My sister had done so previously and she had been given a box to stand on in the pulpit. She was taller than I was so I had to have two boxes to stand on to be seen. I felt so superior. But there was a lot more to it than this ego-recitation. The festival was held on Whit Monday and that meant a new outfit always. My mother knew a seamstress in the village who made our new dresses. She was a Mrs Sarah Bernhard – a name so un-Welsh that it made it all a surreal high-fashion episode. Cenarth village might have been outlandish, but we had our priorities.

There was one more occurrence that made life for my sister and myself more exciting than gliding down the red carpet of the Oscars ceremony today. A lady who lived on the fringe of the village, Miss Edith Davies, Penlan, was the epitome of refined fashion and her sartorial blessing was even more important than the awfulness of forgetting our biblical lines. We paraded up and down the road to her farm until we got the sweeping affirmation, 'Oh. Charming! All in blue' or 'All in pink' or 'All in puce'. Yes, the same words every year, with just a change in our choice of colours. And away we would trot, happy with her approval.

But for me there was something more exciting still regarding our *cymanfa ganu*. In between the singing sessions, I would be taken down to the ruins of the old castle at Newcastle Emlyn. Always strolling around the castle was a very knowledgeable gentleman, David Richard Davies, a printer in the town. I would listen fascinated to his stories about the 14th-century Welsh poet Dafydd ap Gwilym. It was sheer adventure to listen to his stories and hear how Dafydd would visit his uncle who at one time was in charge of the castle. He would describe how the poet lived in those ancient times and quote lines of his intricate poetry. And though I didn't understand half of what he was telling me, I never stopped listening. Years later I was truly grateful to David Richard Davies for instilling into the mind of a child an interest in the remarkable work of one of the great, if not the greatest, of our Welsh poets.

I also listened to his stories about Princess Nest, daughter of Rhys ap Tewdwr. She was my dream princess as a child, ravishingly beautiful, the Cleopatra of Wales. But she was much more than an acclaimed beauty. Each time I see Catherine Zeta

Jones, I see my Welsh Princess. She fought for her lover and her country. She became mistress of Henry I and was ordered by him to marry the Norman oppressor, Gerald of Windsor. She was the grandmother of Gerald the Welshman and through her many love affairs, became the mother of the great Norman-Welsh family, the Geraldines, who conquered Ireland and were the ancestors of the present day Kennedys of America. I really must turn her life into a musical.

Looking back, I seem to think of Newcastle Emlyn always as the place where all the 'extras' had a go at moulding me into shape. I'll try to explain.

The Extras

MUSIC

In my time, we were not taught music at school. My mother had to pay privately for our piano lessons at Newcastle Emlyn. My teacher was Miss Rita Davies, Castle House, a member of the Gorsedd of Bards and always known as Pencerddes Emlyn, which made her the tops – higher than the ordinary *Cerddores* ('musician'). And what a lively extrovert.

I was really, however, into words and not music. Apart from my earlier banjo death wish, I found pounding scales a total misuse of energy. But the Cardi craftiness saved me. I had found out that Miss Davies had a crush on John Bot – our Botany Master at Cardigan Grammar School. A lovely fellow. Luckily for me, in those days, nobody had even dreamt of mobile phones and texting. So I volunteered to carry love notes between my music mistress and botany master. It worked. Compared with the composing of those notes, my scales were way down in importance. You may, of course, think that Rita Davies was negligent as she turned a deaf ear to my wobbly scales. For her guidance, I am eternally grateful.

During a lesson one day, Rita ordered me to write some verses so that she could set them to music. I was about nine or ten years of age at the time so they were simple ideas that came easily and such activity was infinitely better than pumping out discordant notes. I scribbled away and finished quite a few before leaving. Next lesson, I did another lot. The *Pencerddes* looked pleased and was going to compose music for them.

Life went on and I forgot all about them. But Rita and I were destined to meet again.

POETRY

When I gave up music lessons, I found another extra for my mother to subsidise. I wanted to learn *cynghanedd* (the strict-metre form of Welsh poetry). I believe, these days, that it is taught excellently in many secondary schools. I don't think there was anyone in my village interested, so, it was off to Newcastle Emlyn – again – this time to have private lessons with Mrs Davies, the wife of the Baptist minister, Clement Davies. She was an excellent teacher, but a North Walian, so I guess we had a few stumbles on the way. I had fallen in love with the ancient form of an ode when listening to David Richard Davies, my singing-festival friend on the castle grounds. When I was having music lessons, Pencerddes Emlyn was forever pressuring me into sitting the literary exam that would grant me entrance to *Gorsedd y Beirdd*, the Eisteddfod Bardic Circle. I used to attend Mrs Clement Davies's classes, too, in Welsh literature, so, sooner rather than later, I felt proficient enough to have a go. I found that I would have to sit three examinations before I could become a member and wear the ceremonial blue gown that I so admired. Recklessly, as usual, I decided to sit all three in one go. I had to go to Llandysul for this nine-hour marathon – three hours for each paper. When it was over, I don't know which of us felt the greater relief – myself or the poor man supervising me! I felt really guilty when, a little later, the Eisteddfod Board decided that there would be a rule that no one in future could sit three examinations on the same day.

Anyway, I was very lucky and successfully passed the bardic grades. I wore my blue gown with pride when I was much later initiated into the Circle at the Fishguard National Eisteddfod in August 1936, under my bardic name 'Luned Teifi'. Since then, I have only missed two National Eisteddfodau, the ones at Meifod in 2003 and Eryri in 2005, on both occasions because of serious car crashes. For this devotion to our annual national festival, I give weighty credit to Pencerddes Emlyn, my enthusiastic music teacher – and the greatest publicist and optimist I was lucky enough to have known.

My music lessons with the *Pencerddes* came to an end, but not our friendship. She had given up on my Botany master and was now Mrs Alcwyn Evans, a sea captain's wife. Her husband, I think, travelled a lot and piloted ships into ports. Eventually, they moved to London to live. I also finished at Cardigan Grammar School about the same time, and was sent to a London Boarding School. Rita would invite me at weekends to visit her at her home in Rayners Lane. What fun! She had a heart of gold and her home was always packed with Welsh people who were either studying or working around the city. She would make *cawl* to dispel the *hiraeth* in the young hearts feeling lost in that mighty metropolis. There was never a dull moment.

Quite often, Rita and I would dress in Welsh costume and criss-cross the city to give talks on Wales and the Welsh. No opportunity was ever lost. She not only boosted my confidence in facing an audience, but, hopefully, we boosted the Welsh economy as well. Through her, also, I got a real taste of classical music. She would take me to the Madame Payling Concerts. It was there I met Kathleen Ferrier, the unique contralto, along with many other famous singers of the time.

It was Rita also who engineered the publication of my first book – well, actually, half a book. Not wanting to miss a trick, our *Pencerddes* gobbled up the chance of publicity once I had passed my bardic examinations and had the title 'Luned Teifi'. She dusted over the poems I had written during my lessons with her, and had forgotten, and having composed the music for them, presented them to the well-known publishers, Gomerian Press, Llandysul. And so, to coincide with my acceptance into the Bardic Circle, a book for schools appeared: *Caneuon i Blant* ('Songs for Children'). Music by PENCERDDES EMLYN. Words by LUNED TEIFI. It was a total surprise.

Rita, bless her, decided there would be a special *cawl* evening for all her London Welsh friends to celebrate. So we both went out to buy leeks, cabbages and all the good things that every Welsh *Mam* would traditionally combine to make this feast. It nearly landed me in a lot of trouble. We completed our shopping (having found a lovely, round cabbage), but passing by a cinema on the way home, we saw a really exciting film being advertised. We went in. Caught up in the excitement of the plot, we let go of the cabbage and it rolled down under the slope of the centre seats. The cinema was in total darkness, but in no way were we going to abandon such a vital ingredient. So Rita and I went groping for it in the dark. In my frustration, I even grabbed a man's leg – and made things worse by whispering that I was looking for a lost cabbage! The man was getting furious. Thought I was calling him a cabbage (my Welsh accent probably). By this time the attendant was approaching. Luckily, at that moment, Rita, who was searching on the other side, gave a yelp of satisfaction, and held up the cabbage victoriously. The attendant shone the light on it. I think the furious man called me 'You . . . idiot'. I left the cinema a very subdued little *Cardi*. Rita later made a huge feast of cawl, and even a greater feast of the incident.

My London period was great fun, and a growing-up period as unknown avenues opened before me, some of which I would like to re-explore with you.

But in case I forget in all my ups-and-downs in that surprisingly busy 'peaceful' village of Cenarth in the 1930s, I really would like you first to meet Aunty Hannah.

Aunty Hannah

Aunty Hannah was my mother's eldest sister. A little dumpling of a woman but a great favourite with everyone. I wrote a Welsh poem trying to describe her once. It started something like this:

> Bwrlwm o hiwmor iachus
> yn dawnsio o lygaid direidus;
> Wyneb brodiog, cariadus.
> Hen ŷd y wlad heb yr us.

which might roughly translate as

> A bubble of infectious laughter
> dancing in mischievous eyes;
> A face embroidered by the laughter of life.
> The old native grain without the husk.

I wrote another one, more light-hearted, in my homely Cardiganshire dialect; one which invariably provokes calls of *encore* when I give a talk on my favourite aunt.

Aunty Hannah's husband was blind ever since I knew him, but she struggled on farming a smallholding, Coynant, a mile or two from the village of Cenarth. She used to walk her husband every Sunday to his childhood Baptist chapel in Newcastle Emlyn. But whilst her husband proceeded to partake of the Communion, Aunty Hanna had to sit outside. And, as a child, I was really rashly angry when I discovered this. Imagine, Aunty Hannah, who so willingly made it possible for her husband to attend his usual place of worship, was allowed no place within that building! I thought she had been sent out because she had

39

done something against God. When they tried to explain to me that she was a member of a different denomination, I tactlessly told the minister that God should be for all, not only the people he wanted to preach to. Maybe with all my family being Congregationalists, I was born with a highly-evolved ecumenical sense. Or, at least, if I didn't have one before, I developed it on the spot that day.

Aunty Hannah became a joyful addition to the family after her husband died just before the Second World War, but believe me, she was sometimes a handful. If the telephone rang, she was the first to answer, and before we got to any message, she would have questioned the caller and found all about his or her life and formed a bosom friendship there and then! I used to take Aunty Hannah with me whenever I wanted to park awkwardly in any of the local towns so that invariably, when I returned to the car, I would find Aunty Hannah occupying some policeman or other in the most cheerful of chats. She was a bit of a poet and story-teller, too, and this occasionally bordered on being a problem. When I later worked on weekly or daily radio soaps for BBC Cymru, Aunty Hannah would set out to create her own work also. I was always a last-minute worker and there were deadlines – deadlines to be taken seriously. Often at this critical time, she would have her poem or story which had to be shared with me. It should have been an irritation, but, so captivating was her innocent charm, that things generally ended in laughter.

And fair play to Aunty Hannah, I could be a problem to myself without any help from her. I remember a very silly incident. I debated whether I would admit to it, but in an autobiography, I guess the reader would expect the really stupid mishaps as well as the nearly stupid ones. I had been working at the BBC in Cardiff and was having a lift home with one of the cameramen who happened to be filming the other side of Cardigan the next day. We had been friends for years and he was staying at my home that night as he often did when filming in the area. When passing through Carmarthen on the way home, he suggested that he would like to take me to dinner at the Ivy Bush Hotel, as repayment for the many times he had stayed with my family. I said I would have to telephone home – Aunty Hannah was, after all, nearing her century – and if all was well, I would be delighted to accept his offer. We found a telephone box outside the Boar's Head.

All was well at home. I hurried back to tell Bill that my big sister Get had told us to take our time. So I made a leap into the car, and knowing Bill very well, greeted him laughingly, 'All yours for the night, darling.' I expected a jocular response and looked to see why one wasn't forthcoming. I was looking at a complete stranger. I was in the wrong car. I was so embarrassed I leapt out without even apologising. Bill was half out of his car and demanding to know what I had said to the man who was still staring after me. It wasn't a very happy dinner. The man had a table right behind us. Much later, however, we did laugh a lot at my generous offer to a total stranger, but I don't know whether anyone making such a stupid mistake today would have got away with it so lightly. I am sorry for the young, and for the old too, today. The world has become a much more dangerous place to live in.

Now, please, can we forget that embarrassment and get back to Aunty Hannah. She was well known as a rod-and-line angler. She sold her smallholding to come and live in one of the three cottages next to Cenarth Falls. She knew the moods of the Teifi river instinctively. Indeed, experienced anglers would telephone us to find if Aunty Hannah was out fishing. If she was not, they would not bother to come near the river that day.

We are very proud of Aunty Hannah. She is, possibly, the only woman ever to have had a pool named after her on the river Teifi. 'The Hannah Rees Pool', close to the Falls is well known to anglers. Her catches there were astronomical. She was also given the freedom of the Falls area by the owner, Captain Charles Fitzwilliams. I will try to remember the Welsh dialect poem I wrote which sheds a little light on her character, although acknowledging that such translations are, generally, poor substitutes.

AUNTY HANNAH

When the snowdrops dare from the soil to come peeping
and the Wagtail starts her sexy preening,
Aunty Hannah like a young girl of twenty
at the crack of dawn would run down to the Teifi.
And in her hand not a fancy rod to ply
but her own hazel stick from a hedge nearby.

She'd catch the sewin and salmon in hives
and sell to the husbands to deceive their wives.
No one ever saw her catch the throw-back tiddlers.
Aunty Hannah had a secret pocket sewn on to her knickers
and she'd swear that she'd shout until Pharoah could hear
if the Bailiff ventured to search so intimately near.

On the rock beside her an alarm clock would be sitting,
the only master to remind her of her husband's feeding.
At ninety-seven why should a soul worry
if the hours of work had become a bit dodgy.
And every Spring when the lambs would be dancing,
Aunty Hannah would dream a stick from the hedge to go fishing.

She was a famous figure at the Falls for years. She would sit her blind husband in the doorway of her cottage while fishing in her special pool. Morgan, the cat, was always attentive at her side and would carry each catch and place it neatly at Peter's feet. People would come and watch and be amazed that the cat never attempted to eat the fish. Such was her stardom that Aunty Hannah was constantly being photographed by people from all over the world. Indeed, she and I even featured in a film together, 'Troubled Waters', almost at the end of her life. She never seemed to be old. She died in 1968, three months before reaching her 100th birthday.

The only one who could ruffle Aunty Hannah's feathers was the rebellious preacher-poet Dewi Emrys. When he used to stay with us, we always had to confine one of them in a no-entry zone. Both were recognised as incomparable anglers, and when it came to discussing such sophisticated matters as the tying of artificial flies, civil war would never be far away. Both were saddled with what we called in Welsh *Y Fi Fawr* ('the Big I Am'). They were absolute egotists. And, if Cynan, one of the great eisteddfod characters, also happened to be present, it became a world-premier drama.

But more of Dewi Emrys in a minute, and later on.

London, Paris and Cenarth

When I left Cardigan Grammar School, I was sent to London to a boarding school. I'm not quite sure why, but I think the family reasoning was that maybe I would dislike the noisy, wicked city, and would want to come home and settle for going to university and becoming a teacher. My mother's friend, Katie, trying to explain to an inquisitive neighbour, said that I had been 'sent there to be polished off'. Sorry, but the polish was obviously the wrong brand. I didn't shine but, step by step, I entered a life totally different from the one of my home village.

London was magic in those far-off days, all the better for having a close friendship at boarding school with Joan, whose father worked in India. So, she and I were the only two, really, who belonged to other countries. We both agreed that school-work was tedious, and had strong views about not becoming teachers. Joan was more inclined to have a career in music. I still had my heart on becoming a writer.

I was overjoyed to be in a city where Fleet Street was bursting with writers. I had heard so much about this exciting street from people who called at my home – and one of their favourite topics was the Welsh poet, Dewi Emrys (David Emrys James). I always listened in to their debates – and sometimes they were fast and furious. He must have been a true rebel and I was at the age to adore poets, especially rebellious ones. Everybody seemed to agree that he was a great poet but having won the National Eisteddfod Crown at Swansea in 1926, he had pawned it immediately at a local pawnbroker's shop. A fifty-million-pound heist in sleepy Cenarth would have created less of a strangling debate: some admiring and forgiving; some dead against. I listened avidly. I didn't know what crime he had committed. I had never heard of a pawnbroker's shop. I looked up the word 'pawn' in the dictionary. Yes. What he had done seemed a crime. He must have written a good poem to have won a crown, mind. It left me utterly confused for years but I always clung to my mother's reply to all the debaters: 'We musn't judge him. We do not know what circumstances he found himself in at the time'. Oddly enough, when I did get to know him, I read a poem he had written, *'Y Nos'* ('The Night'), that echoed my mother's sentiments exactly.

So, if my mother had a good word for him, that was good enough for me. I heard, too, that he was working in Fleet Street, and before going to London found out the name of the pub he normally frequented.With red-headed recklessness, as usual, I decided that meeting this rebel poet would do more for my writing career than schoolwork would. So Joan and I became apt to play truant. Wearing heavy lipstick and high heels, we would sneak down the fire escape and on reaching Fleet Street would shadow this pub, hoping to meet this inspiring giant. We didn't meet him then, but I did later. I think a rebel poet deserves a chapter of his own, so I'll come back to him again. And, anyway, I was encountering other excitements which weren't meant to be in my school schedule either.

In the 1930s it would take a whole day to come home to Cenarth. The old GWR train would move from station to station with all the rapidity of a pregnant ewe. It would eventually deliver me at Carmarthen station. Then I would go by road to Cenarth, after an elaborate confusion about my train ticket – sometimes I couldn't find it, and sometimes I would have absent-mindedly torn it up and would present a fistful of shredded paper to the Station Master. In the end he would take me into his office to sort me out and give me a cup of tea. The railway men in those days were so kind and helpful.

Even years after I'd left school, I could make myself a bit of a nuisance at Carmarthen station. I held up the train to London once for three-quarters-of-an-hour. And that was not so long ago either. I was going to a conference in Cardiff – all dressed up in my Sunday best and slip-on shoes. There was quite a gap between the train and the platform and on entering, one of my shoes fell under the train. Even if I dared, the place was too narrow to rescue it. I was totally embarrassed. There was no way I could go to my sedate conference hobbling on just one shoe. The train was due to depart, and if I hadn't been the culprit, I would be very vociferous at such a delay. A crowd gathered around me. I thought I saw a forest of umbrellas and walking sticks at the ready. The time dragged on and on and I was sure I was having nightmares in broad daylight. Would it be better to face the appointment with one shoe rather than a battered head? In the end I did reach my goal, somewhat late, but with only my dignity slightly bruised. The cleaner found a long-handled pair of tongs, captured my shoe, but taking no chances, ordered me into the train before putting it on for me. I must confess, even having crossed the ninety age-line, I still love trains.

But, as I started to explain, it took a whole day to go home to Wales but only a few hours to get to Paris. So I think you will agree that anyone young of heart with any free time would opt for Paris. I was so lucky. Joan's brother was a musician over there. So in no time at all, we were welcomed to the Bohemian magic of the Left Bank. I persuaded myself, and those close to me, that this was education with a capital 'E'.

One of our friends over there was Noel, a young composer. He would record his songs, and I would smuggle his records back to London. Probably a bit illegal, but it really did help my meagre allowances. Even when I finished school, Joan and I remained friends so crossing to France became a way of life. In fact I have to admit that, one way or another, this vibrant city, so at odds with my sleepy Cenarth, eventually altered my life. But first let me tell you how luck led me to an unusual and very rewarding friendship.

One night on the Left Bank, with nothing really exciting

going on, Noel asked me whether I would like to meet the greatest singer that France had ever known. Because I was Welsh, everyone always assumed that I was a great singer. Unfortunately not, but I am a lover of all music, so I jumped at the chance of meeting this acclaimed singer.

Off we went to Montmartre, climbed the innumerable steps, and arrived at a very inauspicious apartment. The whole place was in darkness. Noel opened the door. The dampness hit my nostrils. I peered inside and could only see a chair in the middle of the room. From the light of one candle, in the shadows I could see someone sitting in the chair. It looked like an Egyptian mummy. I thought it was a very old, or a very sick person. I noticed that Noel had taken a bottle of wine from his pocket to hand over to this bundle of blackness, and heard him saying that he had brought someone from Wales to visit. By this time I had worked out that I was having my leg pulled.

I turned towards the door, my red hair scorching, and my brain double-speeding the number of inhuman retributions awaiting Noel. I had almost reached my escape door when from the shadows I heard this deep command: '*Arretez*'. I turned in confusion and could dimly see this mummy getting out of the chair and stripping off one black coat, two, three – four black coats. Then she sang.

> Elle est née comme un moineau;
> Elle a vécu comme un moineau
> Elle mourra comme un moineau.

> (She was born like a sparrow;
> She lived like a sparrow;
> She will die like a sparrow.)

I shuddered to a stop. I can still feel the effect – like a load of grit poured down my scorched back. The voice was unique. The voice still is whenever I hear it.

I went back, I suppose, to try to thank her. We talked. She was interested that I was Welsh. There was no apology about the state I had found her in. She simply asked if I could come back and see her in ten days. There was no way I would have said no. And I was back, but this time we met in the Pigalle. She had moved out to a more comfortable apartment. We found an unexpected, but decided, empathy. Not long after, she moved to a flat in the affluent district of the Bois de Bologne, where I was offered an ever-open door, and where I spent some truly treasured hours.

Piaf

I have always known that it was sheer luck that I met Edith Piaf on that momentous night. It took me quite a while to understand how that luck had worked. When she sang, I accepted immediately Noel's description of her as the greatest singer France had ever known. It was obvious that he idolised her and was reluctant to try to explain why we first found her in such poor surroundings. But as I got to know her, I began to understand.

As a child, her father an acrobat, used to take her to sing around the streets of Paris. She had a hard life and always compared herself to the lowly sparrow. I wrote one lyric, *La Môme Piaf* (the French slang for ' the little sparrow'):

> They marked her birthplace near a door
> in rue Belleville, haunt of the poor:
> The little sparrow born to soar.

> She roamed the Paris streets at night,
> the bourgeoisie blind to her plight:
> The little sparrow born to fight.

> She sang her agony of need,
> her rugged voice pitched high to plead:
> The world slinked by at double speed.

> The urchin sparrow learned to fly;
> the sky turned blue, the clouds rolled by.
> She lit a beacon on life's high.

> La Môme Piaf . . . La Môme Piaf.
> The little urchin sparrow.

She sang her heart on the world stage,
She sang her heart, unlocked the cage
and came in from the shadow,
She sang her heart on the world stage
She sang her heart, unlocked the cage
Goodbye, goodbye to sorrow,
  Non, non, rien de rien,
  Non, je ne regrette rien.

I wrote another Welsh lyric also, '*Llwyd Bach y Baw*' (the Cardiganshire slang for a little sparrow). Both lyrics have been set to music by the well-known composer of songs and film soundtracks, Michael J. Lewis, born a *Cardi* but who has for years lived and worked in Los Angeles.

Singing one night on the street, Piaf was discovered by Louis Leplee, owner of the Club Gerney in the city. He saw the great potential and invited her to sing at his club. She became a great success. Then, in 1936, Louis Leplee was murdered. The Gendarmes, probably needing a quick suspect, accused Piaf. She was later cleared but the damage had been done. She had adored Leplee as a father and was lost without his guidance. She fell into a deep depression and, when I first saw her, was evidently under the influence of drugs. Cenarth was a far cry from the drug scene; I had never heard of, or known anybody, taking drugs. The puzzle of my coming back to see her in ten days was solved. She knew that by then, she would be back to her normal self.

Nowadays, drugs are easily available in most countries you visit. Yet, luckily, in all my years of living, I have never felt the need to boost my sense of happiness with drugs, or alcohol, for which I am eternally thankful.

It was a kind of surreal life visiting Piaf in the Bois de Bologne. She had a huge flat but rarely used more than one room. That would be cluttered with glass-top tables, sofas and easy chairs, with cushions and strips of carpet covering the floor, along with luggage pieces ready for a journey, various musical instruments and a magnificent piano. It always oozed comfort and a welcome. To this day, I don't know how I fitted in. But I did. I've always been fascinated by people, and what a varied crowd gathered there: singers, composers, playwrights, actors. Some slept overnight on sofas, or easy chairs and some in more unlikely places, as I was to find out once. Piaf asked me one night to fetch a sheet of music from across the room. I rushed to do her bidding, trampling over a piece of bulky carpet, little expecting to find I had run over Maurice Chevalier who had been sleeping underneath. Coming face to face with the dishy actor, I was shy and embarrassed but it was one of my better mistakes. He had a great sense of humour and we became good friends . . .

The one for whose work I had great admiration, and whom I desperately wanted to be close to, was Jean Cocteau. I still clung to my twelve-year-old's ambition of becoming a great dramatist. And here I was in contact with the genius. It was not to be. I sat at his feet but found him too difficult to follow. He was a powerful thinker and adored Piaf. He kept on telling us that the day the 'little sparrow' died, he would die too. Oddly enough, when she did die in October 1963, Cocteau died two days after her.

I missed out on saying 'Goodbye' at her funeral. I was in America at the time but years after I did have the opportunity to light a candle for her at the church that had refused to accept her for a burial service at the time, but which had had a change of heart later. So, when that good and reliable friend, Gareth Rowlands, BBC producer, took me over for a televised re-tracing of the steps of my *Llwyd Bach y Baw*, we were accepted with respect.

Piaf was buried in the Père La Chaise cemetery. Each time I visit Paris, I visit her grave and recite the little poem I wrote to her while standing at her tomb one day. I also wrote a Welsh version.

You were a flame devouring time in the flesh
in a raging tempest.
Your wick of hope flickered out –
There was no sun, no moon, no stars.

You were a rose in the agony of aftermath,
withering in spite of our sustenance.
Until Death, the unreasonable
bundled you into its greedy soil.

Yet you remain, your exotic voice
kindling our emotions.
Above the tempest, the voice of a nightingale
bursts into a rainbow crescendo
gilding the treasures of memory.
Our Môme Piaf.

A lot has been written about Edith Piaf along the years. Sometimes I hardly seem to recognise the person I used to know. I admit she was a complex person. But through all the hardships of her upbringing, she was religious and held a steady faith. Granted she could be superstitious, too. I remember once turning up at her flat in the Bois de Bologne carrying a green umbrella. She suddenly snatched it and threw it through her large front window. Being a *Cardi*, I was horrified at the expense of replacing the window. Piaf was totally unconcerned, explaining that it would be better to keep the luck inside. I guess she had the temperament of a genius.

Piaf (or *Llwyd Bach y Baw* as she always wanted me to call her), in spite of her wonderful voice, did not have an easy life. Her baby daughter Marcelle died; she herself became blind for a period; the only person she truly loved, Marcel Cerdan, was killed in a plane crash. And in the end she became riddled with arthritis. My only regret is that she was unable, although anxious to do so, to come to Wales – 'the land of song' as she used to call it.

Not only was she an astounding singer, she could have been one of France's foremost actresses too. I shall never forget being invited (sometime at the beginning of the 1950s, I think) to see Piaf acting in *Le Bel Indifferent* at the Theatre Marigny. The play for two people, one of whom says absolutely nothing, was written specially for her by her devoted friend, Jean Cocteau. She acted this monologue of unrequited love with all the emotions of her life experience. Her non-speaking player at the time was her one-time husband, Jacques Pills. It was a magic masterpiece. She did have another go at acting in *La P'tite Lili*, a kind of musical comedy. Sadly I didn't see this performance, which was also a brilliant success.

Perhaps it is not always remebered that she did a lot of good behind the scenes in the French Resistance too. She had the ear of people with the know-how to smuggle nationalists under sentences of death out of the country in those war years. I personally know one person, at least, whose life she saved by her tireless help and endless connections.

And on a lighter note, perhaps it is now that I should share with you one connection I made through her – and one I still remember with awe and utter admiration.

Picasso

I used to know the artist Augustus John in London – and I shall get back to him later in these memoirs. We were good friends but he had an ego at least double the size of a camel's hump. When we used to meet at the Cafe Royal, London, I often had to referee contests between several egotistic men. I became rather browned off and decided to outwit Augustus John. Impatiently, I decided on my strategy. I turned to my friend, Piaf, for help. She knew everybody. At that time Picasso was a name on every tongue; he was the absolute genius. And I knew he had a studio in Paris.

I would ask Piaf if she would make an appointment for me to go to see him. Going back to brag to Augustus that I had met Picasso would flatten his ego for at least a week or so, or maybe even weeks. As I had foreseen, there was no problem. The appointment was made.

As usual, without much forethought, I presented myself at his studio door. It was opened wide. Picasso stood there, a slightly odd character. He had pink trousers, one navy and one yellow sock and the eyes of a CAT-scan. Running quickly through my mind was the unsettling thought that he could see my lunch, hurried so that I would be on time. I was then faced with the inside wall of his studio, covered with all these paintings that looked to me like the muddled result of a three-year-old trying to arrange a jig-saw. Worse still, there were doves hovering all over. At the time I had a haystack of red hair and I was panicking: supposing their claws caught in my hair! I always suspected I was a coward and this was my test. I turned and ran.

Even to this day, I can still hear my grandmother's voice

chiding: 'If you are ever cornered, stand your ground, don't back away'. And in that split second, I realised that her voice was unusually stern – she, after all, set great store by the advice she used to give us. So I decided to turn back to say sorry to this famous artist and, my conscience eased, I could then make a run for it. But before I had time to open my mouth, he barked at me, wanting to know what was on my mind.

Speaking first and thinking second, I blurted out the truth: a Welsh hymn! He looked stunned. I thought he was going to hit me. I guess he expected me to pay homage to his marvellous paintings. I realised that he must be thinking that I was comparing his wonderful work with a Welsh hymn so I had to explain and then get out hopefully in one piece. I explained that the Welsh hymn I had in mind was *'Dwy aden colomen pe cawn'* ('O for the wings of a dove') and I wished that I was with the hymnist, miles and miles away in fact, on the top of Mount Nebo, because Picasso's work there in front of me was so beautiful and intricate, and I was too ignorant to understand any of it. I apologised for intruding and turned to slip away. But he started laughing jovially and grabbed my shoulder to get me inside the studio. He sat me in a chair and made coffee. I began to relax. I think he was sorry for this ignorant girl from the wilds of Cardiganshire. He turned out to be a superhuman being. I forgot he was *the* super artist of the period, and listened avidly to his explanation of his work. The large painting facing me at the door that had made me panic was *Guernica*. He had not long finished it. He explained in detail the idea behind it. And listening to his denouncement of the civil war in his own country, and of the defiling of human beings, I could understand the symbolic nose or an eye in a forehead or navel (or wherever) to portray the results of the insanity of war.

We spent a remarkable afternoon together, going from painting to painting. If he was bored, as surely he must have been, he was too much of a gentleman to show it. It wasn't all plain sailing. I disagreed flamboyantly with him over his painting of what he had called the ugly woman. He had split the face in two – one was reasonable but one side was grotesque. I boldly told him it was an unfair picture. It didn't do me any good. He simply said that it was how I, and every other woman, would look when we reached old age. Today, having reached that stage, I dare not look too closely at myself in the mirror, just in case his brilliant brain had been right there, too.

After the shock of visiting Picasso, it took me a little while back in London to begin the bragging that would deflate my friend, Augustus. But when I did find my courage, I plastered it on thicker than even my old music mistress, Pencerddes Emlyn, could have managed.

Yes. There were mishaps and laughs. But as I wrote once

> Our life's a map of varied shades,
> of sun and clouds and nights of fear . . .
> and trees shed leaves like crying babes.

I cannot leave the Paris scene without remembering those darker shades.

Paris and Per

Paris has been known along the years as the city of lovers. Any one who has walked along the Champs Elysées in the spring sunshine when the chestnut trees are full of bloom, or at night when the flowers are about to close their sleepy eyes, must have felt the blood in their veins dancing with the hope that around the corner could be one's own special joie de vivre. So be it. The unexpected can play see-saw with one's life.

I have never been an enthusiastic party animal, preferring a quiet talk with friends or soft music but the Left Bank was always aglow with invitations and, in Paris, you do as the Parisians do. This night it was a party at Madame Galbrun's.We were having a cheerful time, as usual, when this tall stranger walked in through the open door, playing a clarinet and humming a Welsh tune. I was so surprised. I guess he saw my eyes bulging with wonder, and came straight across to me. We talked almost all night and spent every other moment we could in each other's company. He was a Breton called Per living outside Rennes. He spoke Welsh, having learnt it from a man originally from Llandeilo, who had been working in his village and who had given Welsh lessons to a few interested students. He had graduated as a scientist and had been working in Berlin as a scientific correspondent. This was 1938 and we spent all the time we could together, whenever we both could be in Paris at the same time. He was sometimes uneasy, as there were rumblings of war in Germany underneath the surface. We discussed Wales and Brittany. We had so much in common. Our two countries had so many obvious similarities. Per was an ardent Breton Nationalist. I was also a Welsh Nationalist in those days but never really politically active in Wales, although

I did chair Megan Lloyd George a few times in the days she was canvassing for a Parliament for Wales, and another time tramped around extolling the virtues of the League of Nations. I had the innocence to believe that talking would save the world. Howell Davies, Aberdwylan, one of my chapel's deacons and I nearly came to blows over it.

As time went on, the bond between Per and me strengthened and I knew that it was not the impetuousness of a redhead that decided that here was my soul-mate. Per was equally certain. When a declaration of war was too imminent for me to stay longer in France, Per and I made a vow on parting that even if we found it too difficult to communicate, we would meet again as soon as armistice was declared.

With the optimism of the young, we did not foresee the complications ahead.

We will leave the Breton connection for the time being for, before meeting Per, there was plenty to occupy me in London from the time I left school until the time war was declared. And I was still bent on becoming a writer.

Of Poets and Artists

It was August 1936. I was home for a break from London and feeling mighty pleased with myself. I had that morning been accepted into the Bardic Circle of the National Eisteddfod of Wales, having passed my examinations, and had proudly marched in my blue gown in the procession. I did, as I have done for years and years since, stroll with interest around the *Maes* ('Eisteddfod field') and have a good *clonc* ('chat'). Not the 'Ooh! Look at Jane Ann – all that flesh' or 'Martha May – same old frock this year again' type of talk, but the re-energising of batteries in superior discussions of how to make Wales a vibrant nation etc. Suddenly, my eyes became glued on a group of three men standing below me. I was fascinated – there was an aura. The two tall men, handsome too, were to all purposes having an argument. One had a hat on that wobbled slightly as he tried to iterate his side of the argument. The other had the long white hair of a poet, way over his shoulder, and the shuddering of those locks testified to an equally vigorous advocacy of his side. The stumpy, younger, curly-headed one in the middle looked into space as if expecting salvation from above. I really was intrigued by them. My sister would probably tell me off for being rude, but I just had to find out who they were, so I nudged a man standing near me. I asked if he knew the three men. I was lucky. He seemed eager to tell me: 'Of course I know them. I'm a Pembrokeshire man. They, too, are Pembrokeshire men -- well, the two tall ones are, and the little one is as good as being.'

I pressed him for names. He proudly obliged. The tall man wearing a hat was Augustus John, the artist, well known around Tenby; the other tall one was Dewi Emrys, the poet born in

Pencaer – quite near, and the small, chubby one was Dylan Thomas, also a young poet, and much talked about at the time. What luck. What an inspiring trio! I was too young and shy to approach them. My main concern was Dewi Emrys, the man I'd been stalking along Fleet Street when playing truant. I spent my whole Eisteddfod week finding answers. I discovered that the three, at the time, were friends and living in London. I was ecstatic and impatient to get back to the bustling city. I contacted Joan and persuaded her to join me in stalking the rebel poet again. We did find him but I was still too shy to approach him. In the end, it was Joan who had the courage to accost him and introduced me. That started a long and rewarding friendship, which started with my telling him how I had been impressed on seeing three such important men together at the Fishguard National Eisteddfod, so he arranged for me to meet the three together again at the Cafe Royal, where they frequently met. After all these years I still have a warm corner in my heart for that memorable eisteddfod at Fishguard.

The Cafe Royal
and Augustus John

To someone from Cenarth, the Cafe Royal in my younger days was not a home from home. It appeared to me to be forever bursting with odd, creative geniuses, like Edith Sitwell. I was in awe of her, but also had a somewhat envious admiration of her courage in bellowing out her poetry to all and sundry through the hugest old-fashioned gramophone trumpet I'd ever seen. She appeared to have a cast-iron self-defence against the world. No doubt it was Dewi Emrys's concern for my welfare that kept me, almost compulsively, hinged to this mottled crowd.

One of Dewi Emrys's first favours was to introduce me to Augustus John, the artist. I had heard of him and his sister, Gwen, both artists and Welsh born. He, apparently, then was well known for his romantic pursuit of younger women. Even today, when Augustus's name crops up, there are arched eyebrows and open mouths waiting for some sordid kiss-and-tell tales to be boastfully acknowledged. There never were any. Augustus John and I became genuine friends.

I think there were simple reasons for this. I had been introduced by Dewi Emrys, who was his friend, but who was also taking fatherly care of this lonely girl from Wales. Another fact was that my mind was completely taken over by Per, my clarinettist, and I hardly even noticed anyone else. But above all, the knowledge that my grandmother had been midwife to the gypsies was a trump card. Our talks always centred on the Romany families that we were both interested in. In the end it turned out that he did not have Romany blood in his veins, as he usually loudly proclaimed. And it was Dewi Emrys himself who opened my eyes to this.

These two new friends of mine, the poet and the artist, had the biggest egos that I had ever encountered. Both were forever debating, both furiously stubborn almost to the point of blows. Most times, to avoid scenes, I would have to referee between them. One night the topic was gypsy blood. Augustus John was in high voice bragging his Romany connections. Dewi Emrys, whose circumstances at times had forced him to take to the roads, literally, rounded on him. 'Stop your bragging, man. You have not a drop of Romany blood in your veins.' The artist's refutation of this insult against his pedigree came thundering: 'Listen, poet. I am of the Petulengro family, a well-known Romany tribe.' Dewi looked down his classical nose: 'You may well be, my friend, but as you know, Petulengro is only a translation of the common name Smith, no more belonging to the Romany clan than my name, James.' With a mischievous salute to the poet, we heard no more bragging of being a gypsy, but Augustus John and I still went on discussing our interest in these special roaming families.

And how I listened to his anecdotes, especially the gypsy ones and his description of characters as only seen through the eyes of an artist. There was one special friend that crept every time into our talks. He was the gypsy scholar, John Sampson, whom everyone knew as The Rai. Augustus and John had met in Liverpool, where Augustus, after marrying Ida Nettleship, had taken a teaching post at the School of Art, which was affiliated to the University College. John Sampson was the Librarian there. Hearing of this scholar and his interest in gypsies, and knowing that he and teaching would never be bedmates, Augustus made a beeline for this gypsy-lover and, in no time, he and The Rai became close friends. John Sampson soon taught him the Romany dialect and took him to the local gypsy camps.

Sampson was a giant. He spoke perfect Romany and had acquired the secret jargon of the tinkers with their back and rhyming slang, and later added learning Sanskrit to his many achievements. He experimented in verse and translated Heine, Fitzgerald and others into Romany. His edition of William Blake is regarded as exemplary and definitive. Augustus never tired of telling me about the outrageous times he and The Rai had at the Cabbage Hall Camp, a large patch of waste ground outside Liverpool where the Boswells (my old friends too) used to encamp during the winter. I was fascinated and one of my deepest regrets is that I never met this great friend of Augustus John. But I always felt that I knew The Rai intimately, for the eye of the artist moulded him to perfection – the wayward hair, baggy trousers, old velvet jacket, muff, gin bottle, the battered slouch hat at an imposing angle, and the eternal fag at the corner of his mouth clinging on obediently through all the gypsy anecdotes.

Augustus John was delighted that I took so much interest and was constantly showing me his acclaimed frontispieces to Sampson's publications – *Omar Khayam* (1902); *Wind on the Heath* (1930); *Romani Gilia, John Sampsoneste* (1931); *Portrait of Sampson, for the Gypsy Lore Society* (1928), and his caricature of Sampson when president of the Society. He also produced a self-portrait for the Jubilee issue, demanding that the cover was produced in the Romany colours of black, red and yellow. I have no doubt at all that John Sampson had a great influence on the artist's life.

John Sampson died in November 1931 and I heard many times how Augustus had been invited to read the Rites at the ceremonial scattering of his friend's ashes and to recite The Rai's chosen verses from his Romany translation of Fitzgerald's *Omar Khayam*. As Augustus told it, stretched ego-wise or not, it must have been an electrifying performance by him from memory. I can vouch for the effect, for he repeated the verses to me more than once, with perfect diction and memory intact.

Looking back and trying to cope with these reminiscences, I find myself not only surprised, but in utter awe of the fact that I managed to fit in so comfortably on the occasions I met Augustus John. I was barely twenty when we first met and he was somewhere in his fifties and a well-known portrait painter. Maybe our only point of contact was our wayward impulsiveness of acting first and getting into complications after. Augustus was certainly a free spirit. When sometimes he would talk of his boyhood, you could almost feel his frustrations. He lost his mother when he was six years of age and he and his father had an unbridgeable communication chasm. Edwin John would never admit that anyone in his family held a position below the status of a professional lawyer. Augustus would trot out a jingle sometimes, something like

> Lawyers, lawyers everywhere
> and not a highway man in sight . . .

I wish I could remember it all. I guess it would have given an insight into the life of a young boy with artistic inclinations trying to wriggle free from the apparent snobbishness of the time, or, at least, of his father's outlook.

After his mother died, two aunts were supposedly looking after him. He found them an utter embarrassment. Augustus vowed that 'the bossy aunts took over to save me and the world. Their damned "Hallelujah Chariot" chased all over the Tenby streets remonstrating and rescuing drunks and I would finally be dragged into the chariot and made fun of by the street boys who were forever following.'

He summed up his childhood as one 'over-exposed to religion'. His empathy with gypsies probably started there. He always said that his first real painting was 'a sneak peep through a gap in the hedge overlooking a gypsy camp outside Tenby town – a pageant of life.'

As children, the artist and his sister Gwen were regimentally marched to church every Sunday where their father played the organ. On the way there, Edwin John would only raise his hat to

My grandfather

'Mam', my grandmother.

Aunty Hannah

Glanawmor, the family home in Cenarth.

Glyn-y-Mêl, my retirement bungalow built across the road from Glanawmor.

1976. The family with Mary Lloyd Evans (second from right, front row) visiting from the USA.

Aunty Hannah in the thatched summerhouse at Glanawmor.

Have coracle, will travel.

(photo: Jason Thomas)

My chapel, Bryn Seion.

Gwallter Ddu,
the Rev. D.D. Walters.

The Rev. Wynford Thomas M.Th.,
my present minister.

The celebrated brothers and preachers, Justin and Herber Evans, both sons of Bryn Seion.

The Mill at Cenarth Falls. *(photo: Andrew Gilbert)*

Dewi Emrys

With Gareth Rowlands (BBC), filming at Dewi Emrys's memorial stone at Pwllderi.

Fforddolion Ceredigion ('The Cardiganshire Wayfarers')

Y Bwthyn, Dewi Emrys's home in Talgarreg.

Teulu'r Mans, the popular radio show, starring Dilys Davies (Mersi Fach) and Manny Price (Joe Long).

The great snow of 1947 with big sister Get, and the Bretons, Albert and Robert.

Dylan Thomas by Augustus John.

Edith Piaf.

Edith Piaf's grave at Père La Chaise in Paris.

a passer-by of professional standing. The two youngsters would carry their drawing blocks with them everywhere. Gwen would spend her time in church drawing serious subjects. Augustus, on the other hand, would invariably draw caricatures. This would often get him into trouble. Indeed, he always insisted that the stone deafness in his left ear was the result of a hefty blow by one of his masters at school when he discovered a wicked caricature of himself.

Luckily for Augustus John, his father rated artists; they were almost level with lawyers, so he was allowed to escape to the Slade, the prestigious London School of Fine Art, hoping to become a member of the Royal Academy rather than a high-ranking officer in the army, as his father would have preferred. Out of such freedom was born the Augustus that most of us remember – the flamboyant portrait painter.

I guess I cannot, or should not, disregard what has been a debating point along the years and even to this day: was it that infamous crack on the head that changed Augustus's personality from the quiet, almost shy person at the Slade? The story goes that he and Gwen (who had also been accepted there) were home for a short holiday. They were strolling on the Tenby seashore with a friend and their father when Augustus, on a sudden impulse, ran quite a distance from them to his favourite bathing spot at Giltar's Point. Stripping and diving into the sea, he knocked his head on a concealed rock. When his father and the others caught up with him, they found him a complete mess of bloodied nakedness trying to tie a towel round his head to staunch the river of blood. His father was highly embarrassed. What would his professional peers think? He demanded that Augustus should be helped back home – but through the back streets. Augustus would always mimic his father in telling the story: 'Short of death, publicity at all costs should be avoided.'

I remember asking Augustus if it really was the crack on the head that had forged the flamboyant, egotistic character that we knew. His answer was typically Augustus: 'No damned fear. It was the beef tea, Welsh girl. Recuperating with brown beef tea, brown walls, brown furniture and brown, brown thoughts.' Then, after a long draw on his pipe, 'If you must have a reason, it was probably the smoker's cap. Bright, over-the-rainbow colours, with prominent tassels. My father pressed it on my head, on leaving, to hide the bandages, the only way he knew to express his fatherly affection.'

The scene was inevitable. Augustus John, the Welsh boy at the Slade, with his odd-looking cap among the artistic students of varied cultures. It was only a short step to those enormous dangling golden earrings and the gallantry that went with them. Some of the platitudes he delivered willy-nilly with conviction were also, I guess, to hit back: 'Moral sentiment corrupts the young; children are the first to lose their innocence; artists the second; idiots never' and his favourite 'An artist must always have an intimate knowledge of his subject before he can claim to produce a true portrait'.

Growing out of my countrified Cardiganshire upbringing, I realised later that this was probably a cover-up for his well-known bedding of the many high-class ladies who had always been more than willing to participate. I can only ever remember him complaining of difficulties with regard to his male sitters.

There was Field Marshal Montgomery, for instance. He interrupted his sittings more than once because of being called back to duty. Then he wanted to meet Bernard Shaw so Augustus brought Shaw to the studio and sat him opposite Monty, who had been carefully posed on the dais, so that Augustus could paint while the great men talked. Shaw launched forth on a disquisition lasting over two hours. Monty, listening to Shaw's philosophic sociology, completely lost his pose. The artist had to give up all thought of finishing the portrait.

Another portrait that had to be abandoned before completion was that of Lloyd George. I don't think Augustus was over-fond of our great man of Wales. When I was telling him once that my grandmother adored Lloyd George for giving her a pension of two shillings and sixpence, his reply was a grunt: 'That restless Welshman – had a burning arse'. Was there a touch of envy in the insult, however? Was the ex-Prime Minister's prowess in a certain field denting Augustus' own amorous capabilities?

In the time I knew Augustus John, he was always the life and soul of any party. Private conversations were rather rare. There were, though, one or two that I have always remembered. One was on the anniversary of his wife Ida's funeral. It was a sad confession and I felt honoured to be chosen to listen. The sadness was bitingly genuine. His wife had been ill in a Paris hospital. Augustus stayed with her day and night until she died. They toasted each other in Vichy water until she became too weak to hold on. When the final parting struck, he admitted becoming a loser and got drunk for days. He missed her funeral. He neither remembered the date nor the place of burial in time. The distant remembering was a pain of regret that would remain his burden forever.

There was also another night when he was not his usual egotistic, joyful self. He was obviously troubled and needed to unburden himself. I happened to be there and I think he rated me as a good listener. I did listen intently but did not quite grasp the reason for his unusual turmoil. He kept on insisting that he was no longer a great painter. He had been to an exhibition of his and his sister Gwen's paintings, and every critic there seemed to imply that Gwen's paintings were superior to his. He repeated and repeated 'When I am dead I shall only be known as the brother of Gwen John, the acclaimed painter.'

I thought somebody had trodden on his ego and told him to stop his self-pity. He merely added that he had known for some time that he had lost his artistic grip. Then he confessed how he had walked in on his wife Ida and his mistress Dorelia in the flat they had taken over in Paris, and found them kissing. His world had broken apart. How could he ever accept that the two most important women in his life preferred a lesbian attachment?

I had been brought up in conventional, uneventful Cenarth and the word lesbian was almost foreign. I did not wake up to the fact that real life was not always straightforward until some time later when I found myself working in police courts and a mother from my own district came to me to plead for her son who was before the magistrates for a homosexual misdemeanour. I began to understand that to Augustus John, who prided himself on his absolute manhood, the discovery that the two women in his life were lovers made him believe he was a lesser man and that had indeed damaged his artistic talent.

Whatever the critics pronounce on the work of Augustus John, I, and very, very many others will agree that we did lose a legendary and flamboyant character when he died in 1961.

Dylan Thomas

I should have liked him, for I find most of his work truly inspiring. But I did not. The many times I met him, he was too drunk to hold a proper conversation. Perhaps, because I mainly met him in the company of Augustus John, I found him to be, more or less, a scrounger. I thus felt embarrassed. I have always abided by my mother's strict command – if I wanted something, I had to wait until I could afford to pay for it.

One night, the artist was liberal as usual. Dewi Emrys had had his glass of Crème de Menthe from Augustus, and Dylan had been refilled many times. I happened to be standing near the artist when he called the waiter for the bill. He studied it for some time, looking puzzled, then called for an explanation. It was for £250 – a lot of money in those days. The waiter explained about the drinks and that Dylan had also added his bill, board and lodging at the hotel for over a fortnight. Augustus just muttered quietly 'Ah! The boy' and thanked the waiter courteously before turning to his friends to ask if they could lend him some money. I still remember poor Dewi Emrys offering the few shillings he had in his pocket. Augustus, generous to a fault, would not dream of taking it, but had spotted his American agent sitting in the corner and crossed over to bargain with him for the amount needed, promising to leave his latest painting with him as a security until he paid it back.

There was another reason why I found it difficult to be friendly with my birth-mate, Dylan. He didn't particularly wish to be known as a Welshman unless somebody of significant importance from Wales, or with distinguished Welsh connections, happened to be present. I think perhaps this was because he didn't seem to have a command of the language, and possibly felt inadequate. Because I was never comfortable in his company, for years I was reluctant to admit to my date of birth, October 27,1914, because everybody would then know that I had been born the same day as Dylan Thomas. It wasn't until my ninetieth birthday that the Americans finally broadcast it to me and the whole world.

I hope I will never allow my dislike of Dylan as a person to detract from my appreciation of his work. I think most of it is brilliant. I confess some of his work does not appeal and I freely admit that the reason for that is my lack of understanding of some of his themes. I greatly admire his humour and his continuous energy in producing so much published work in so short a life. Deep down, now that the Americans have disclosed our shared date of birth, I am happy and honoured to struggle on in his shadow.

Chasing my Dream

The 1930s were busy years for me in London. This was my time of being a proper writer, the 'starving in a garret' period, essential if I was to realise my dream. I had taken a flat in Bayswater – well, actually, a room in an attic. The rafters almost touched my nose. I guess it was the cheapest I could find in the city, but I had the most warm-hearted, never-to-be-forgotten Irish landlady. Next door, in a similar attic room, was Norma from New Zealand, and, like poor mice, we soon huddled together. With reckless determination, I planned to make Wales proud of her writing genius. Of course I didn't let on back home that I intended to produce Mills-and-Boon-like romantic throw-offs. I had been nurtured on higher things. As a child, my three constant reading companions were the Bible, the Complete Works of Shakespeare and the Complete Plays of Bernard Shaw. Those were the readily available books in the house. After all, it was because of their influence that I had had such a glowing adjudication for that 'Fall of Jerusalem' play that had launched my ambition as a writer in the first place.

I planned a great life of fame. Norma Next Door aided and abetted, becoming my agent. Swank! I've never had an agent since, which looking back, has been a mistake since my business experience is as lacking as my sense of direction was at birth. Down in a flat below us, there was a kind, approachable Austrian refugee, Franz. He lent me his typewriter. We were more or less in business. There was one snag – paper had to be bought with money. My agent was adamant. No scraps of paper and typing on backs of correspondence received. We were lucky. Down further below us again was Sven Lundstedt. His father had a paper factory in Sweden and Sven could supply us with biggish amounts of rejects. We optimistically felt ourselves a commercial entity.

I furiously wrote my first long story. Passed it over to Norma. Some time later, I found the first-born story returned with a rejection slip. It did nothing for my confidence; in fact it dented and bruised it. But there was one good thing about having red hair: depressions were rarely nurtured. I gave Norma another story to be mailed. My agent was very supportive. It came back. Now my ginger genes were indomitably aroused. So I fell back on the old Welsh adage 'Three chances for a Welshman.' It had worked for me in the past and each time it did, I believed in it. Norma stamped the third attempt and sent it. I got a reply. It looked depressingly like the others. I opened it without any stress on my heart beats.

There should be a warning sign outside all envelopes delivering unexpected good news. A cheque fluttered out. It was for three guineas. Three pounds, three shillings. A fortune in those times before the purge of decimalisation nearly returned us all to the workhouse. I flew to tell Norma, my clever agent. Well, I might as well have done, for my feet did not touch the landing. The stairs were at such an awkward angle that I missed and bumped down two flights. Knocked the stuffing out of me. Found out afterwards that I had dislocated my shoulder.

When I could focus again, I saw a man standing over me. Well, actually, I only saw two expensively-trousered legs, until I managed to twist my painful neck round. And yes, I did see that he had a head also. I blew my top. I knew I was a silly girl but in Wales at least we had Good Samaritans to help such girls out. I told him in English, Welsh and French – probably in all three bungled together – what I thought of him. I think he was trying to apologise. What I needed, though, was some physical help to move. I think he went to report to the landlady, for I did get help in the end. Got a very stern telling-off, too. I guess if I hadn't been so selfishly trying to remember all the non-dictionary words that my mother's friend Katie used to bellow out in a temper, I would have heard the man explaining his plight. It was physically impossible for him to bend down as he had an artificial leg, and in those days medical marvels were not nearly as advanced as they are today. I went to apologise and found him to be a really pleasant gentleman – a very able (no joke intended) Lloyds broker. He was intrigued at the words I hurled at him but I did not let on that I actually was too rurally backward to know their meanings.

I would have been quite happy to continue living precariously off my on-and-off writing. My family still wanted me to go to university. My sister had been at Aberystwyth and now had a post as a bacteriologist in Staffordshire. Oddly enough, Dewi Emrys was against my garret-room ordeal. He wanted me to have a sound grounding in education first, and then to feel free to try other creative modes. If only someone had thought of 'gap' years in my time – they sound so respectable.

I didn't want to leave London. It provided easy access to Per across the Channel, after all. So, as luck would have it, I managed to enrol for a while in a journalistic college. I should really explain that piece of luck. I've hesitated in telling you because even for me this was a truly big embarrassment. But the quality of mercy is still not strained, I hope, when you get to my age.

I have an obsession with bookshops. I think I was in Foyles, London, this particular day. It was nearly closing time and by mistake I took the lift down to the basement. It was rather a gloomy place but I couldn't get the lift to return up. I could see another man in the shadows beyond me. He shouted to me not to worry and that the lift would decide to move in its own time. When he moved out of the shadow, I could see that he was dressed in an old frock-coat. I had only seen one of its kind once before and that was on an old tramp at home; one given to him by a wealthy Samaritan to keep him warm. This man had probably been given his and I felt a little annoyed that he hadn't taken better care of it for it was covered in cigarette ash. He had white scraggy hair and a cigarette hanging permanently from the side of his mouth, even when he spoke. He said the basement was the only place he could keep his papers. I was convinced he was one of London's homeless and felt sorry for him. I told him I knew of a hostel for the homeless in the city, run by a Welshman and was certain I could get him in. He produced an odd noise somewhere between a laugh and gurgle of suffocation. Then the lift decided to move. When we got out he patted me on the shoulder and told me to take great care. I did not get a chance to talk to him again. Somebody dragged him hurriedly away.

Later that night I was talking to Augustus John and Dewi Emrys and telling them of this curious character I had met and was really sorry that I had failed to help him. Augustus asked me to describe him. I started telling him about the frock-coat and the hanging cigarette, when both burst out laughing. Still laughing, Augustus chortled 'All Fleet Street should hear of this.' I was beginning to get angry at their lack of sympathy, when Augustus asked me 'Have you ever met Hannan Swaffer?' I told him angrily that everyone knew of Hannan Swaffer, the legend of Fleet Street, but of course I had never actually met him. 'You have now!' was the retort.

Up until then, I had only known Hannan Swaffer by name. And I couldn't believe how I had misjudged and embarrassed this famous Fleet Street magnate. Admittedly an eccentric, he was probably the greatest journalist of all time. He started on the *Daily Mail* and worked under Lord Northcliffe; he wrote for papers like the *Daily Herald*, *Daily Mirror*, and *Sketch*. He also edited *The People*, and was drama critic for *The Daily Express*. He was actually thrown out of quite a number of theatres because of his acid criticism. What is more, he was in three or four films and appeared on *The Brains Trust*. A very active socialist, he was also a well-known spiritualist.

The next day I went in my shame to apologise to this genius

for my faux pas. I would like to boast that he became a great friend but that would be to stretch the truth – and that would never do. He was friendly, though, and took an interest in spite of his varied commitments, in my apparently unintelligent ways. He was known by all as the 'Pope of Fleet Street' and the only reference he ever made to my embarrassing mistake was 'I think I prefer to be known as the "Pope" rather than the "Tramp" of Fleet Street.' He was a fascinating and kind man. He went out of his way to introduce me to the head of a journalistic college and I might have become a proper journalist had not a newspaper baron from China happened to come along looking for a reporter to take up a post on a weekly paper, the *Shanghai Express*. My itchy feet did a continuous tap-dance. He was looking for a man but I could hear my grandmother's 'Go for it girl' and I blinded him with my keenness and Celtic background. I think my stubborn streak played in my favour, too. We bowed, and bowed again and shook hands on an agreement. I had worked it out. It was no longer 'if' but 'when' the war with Germany started. Then there could be no communication with Per, so I could spend some time in China. I went home with the exciting news. A round-table conference was hastily arranged. Uncle Griff had been summoned. I knew then it was serious. There was a unanimous 'No' to my going to China. There was a war there, too.

I *pwdi*ed (Cardiganshire dialect for 'sulking'). I went to North Wales for some mountain air until my mother telephoned: 'Come home before the war is declared. It will not be an easy one.' I knew and went home.

When War Broke Out

There was time for one more hasty trip across the Channel. Unavoidable and unfinished business. Hand in hand, Per and I walked along the Champs Elysées. Not really believing, but with the stubbornness of youth, absolutely refusing to accept that our separation would be a long one. We sealed our plans. Per knew he would be roped in as a war correspondent. I, knowing I would be called to serve, would volunteer to be a Red Cross ambulance driver in France. I rattled off the reasons why I would be accepted. They sounded sound. With impudent confidence, we settled on meeting the moment the war was over. Then we would continue our personal slanging match over which of our respective countries would have the first Parliament,Wales or Brittany?

What degree of topsyturvyism can one humanly accommodate? Nothing, but absolutely nothing, went according to plan. Yes, Germany had marched into Poland and we were at war and everyone foresaw the rationing etc. Everyone tried to plan ahead. However, we suspected – and it was later confirmed – that my mother was in the early stages of Parkinson's disease. But she remained a remarkable planner.

We had a pigsty but had not intended to rear a pig; it had been tried before and on each occasion the pigs had become friends and ended up being given to my Uncle Griff who farmed in a big way. My mother, remembering the 1914-18 war, said there would have to be bacon for the family. So we bought a pig by arrangement with Katie Cilfod. By this time Aunty Hannah was widowed and living with us. My mother also visualised friends from the cities and towns coming to stay with us for breaks in sleepy, peaceful Cenarth. Little did we expect the aeroplane that very nearly landed on top of our house. But more of that later.

Our boys and girls enlisted, one by one. We had formed a committee and had drawn up the boundaries of our village in order to keep in touch with those who had joined the services. Our chair was Johnny Jones, Argoed Farm. A popular, inspirational choice. He could damp down the flames of my red head, however raging. So I felt safe and took over as secretary. There would be Welcome Home concerts for all. We foresaw sugar rationing so I volunteered to keep bees. I knew nothing about bees but we had a big garden and a big orchard and I had heard my mother's cousin, who lived in a bungalow across the road from us, speaking fascinatingly about his beehives. He was a millwright and almost totally deaf but I instinctively knew I could make him hear if ever I was in distress about my bees. Not one of my family took sugar in their tea, so at the end of the war, I was very proud that with the help of the Government's bee-sugar subsidy also, we managed to sweeten the lives of all home on leave.

One way or another, things were settling down in the village. Evacuees came from the vulnerable cities and were billeted at various warm-hearted households. We missed out. Glanawmor, my home, was full of relatives and guests from the South Wales valleys, along with my mother and Aunty Hannah, elderly and needing care. I had informed the authorities of my availability to join the Red Cross ambulance service in France and with as much patience as I could muster, was daily awaiting my call-up. I should, however, have been used to the unexpected.

One day, I took my confusing thoughts to our haven when we were young, the top of the Frenni Fawr, one of the peaks of the Preseli mountain range in next door Pembrokeshire.

I left my car on the Bwlch-y-groes side and walked up. I savoured the freedom for a couple of hours and then knew I had to leave since I had promised my mother I would be home early.

I wended my way down to Bwlch-y-groes. But where was my car? Then reality struck. I suddenly realised I was not at Bwlch-y-groes at all, but at Crymych, miles away. My no-sense of direction had once more led me astray. Luckily, Welsh people are always willing to help; yes, even help fools like me. I found someone ready to re-unite me with my abandoned car. Needless to say, I was a little late arriving home.

My mother was anxiously waiting for me. She had had a visitor looking for me. He was a friend, Roy Evans, a magistrate's clerk from Newcastle Emlyn. I knew his name. Everybody did. He was well known as a leading defence solicitor, with a razor-sharp brain. He had heard, it seems, that I was home from London and as his partner, Jack Nell, had been called to serve in the Army, he wanted me to go to work for him. I thought it was a useless visit since I had had no legal training, but my mother insisted that I should go to see him. I was a bit distracted after my mountain experience, and said, in order to please my mother, I would call on him in the morning. But my mother, who had a great respect for Roy Evans, insisted that he had said that he wanted to see me whatever time I arrived home. Thus it was that I arrived at his home, Brynmarlog, a little before midnight. I told him bluntly that I would be useless as I had no office or legal training. He manipulated the conversation and I understood, there and then, how hopeless it would be if I were ever unfortunate enough to have to face him across the courtroom. I found myself agreeing to meet him at his office in Bridge Street, Newcastle Emlyn, at 9.30 the following morning. I again found my reasonable excuses wilting under his attack. I hastily offered a compromise. I would come and help him for three weeks. In the meantime, he could advertise for a legally-trained person. I asked him when he wanted me to start. The answer was electric. Now!

I had never been inside a magistrates' court in my life. Roy Evans was in charge of three: Newcastle Emlyn, Llandysul and Pencader. And also of two county courts, the ones at Newcastle

Emlyn and Cardigan. That particular morning it was the Newcastle Emlyn Magistrates' Court.

We arrived. The boss and I sat at a table. The Press with business-like notebooks and waving pencils, sat behind. And behind them, quite a crowd of people. Were there so many criminals around this quiet town? I later found out there would always be an audience in these courts. They became evidently a kind of theatre for the areas. In Pencader, especially, it would not be surprising to find up to a hundred people gathered there. Often to witness moments of genuine comedy! Genii are often known to be restless until they are in full commitment. Roy Evans was severely deaf, and in those days a hearing aid was enclosed in a huge box to be carried on the person. It worked perfectly when left alone. Before starting each proceeding, however, the magistrate's clerk would meddle with his hearing-aid box. The intestines would inevitably tumble to the floor. He would bend his head to reach them. I would bend mine to help. We would knock our heads together. Much to the amusement of the onlookers. This happened throughout the time I was in this unusual job.

My first day in court was a remarkable eye-opener. I was sitting beside this brilliant brain, who would spit out a legal inconsistency with the speed of lightning at any poor misguided solicitor. I found the cross-examination of witnesses fascinating, and had the opportunity of taking part at times if there was no solicitor defending. Later I am sure, if I had not still been keen on a writer's career, I would have taken up law and become a barrister.

Suddenly, without warning I was thrown in at the deep end. An affiliation case came up. It was obvious that the girl in the case was not comfortable speaking English. This was before it became compulsory to have professional interpreters in every court. Roy Evans was on his feet, addressing the magistrates and introducing me as a member of the Bardic Circle of the National Eisteddfod of Wales and proceeding to swear me in as an interpreter. I didn't know the jargon in an affiliation case in English, let alone Welsh! The girl was represented by Alun Thomas, a brilliant local solicitor and quite a friend of mine. The opposition was a barrister from Swansea. I caught Alun's eye. There was a definite mischievous wink. But someone, somewhere must have been sorry for me. I grappled with phrases that were not in common usage in English or Welsh. I don't think anyone in that court could distinguish between my red hair and my tortured red face. I found out afterwards that Alun and the barrister had quickly put their heads together to find really, difficult intimate questions to add to my embarrassment. Later his sly trick cost him a few dinners when he became Chief Prosecuting Solicitor for the City of Cardiff and I happened to be working at the BBC, Park Place, Cardiff.

But that instantaneous-translating experience turned out to be the best thing that could have happened. It gave me the confidence to tackle any other cases where help was required. I acted in county courts sometimes, too. Indeed, I became quite a favourite with Judge Temple Morris and he would send for me whenever an interpreter was needed.

I sincerely believe that those six extended years in police courts during the war did more for my career in writing than any college or university could ever achieve. You saw life in all its aspects. You saw the little oddities in people's thoughts. Amazingly, it was often those unfortunate persons who had been caught out in trifling offences, like riding a bicycle without a light, or failing to stop at a crossing, who were the ones to worry, and would beg, sometimes almost on their knees, to be kept out of the papers. The ones with serious cases against them, and there were many, didn't seem to care. In a way, it was a rude awakening for me. Because of Roy Evans's severe deafness, and his absent-minded meddling with his aid-box, I had to be prepared for all contingencies. Every night I had to take Stone's Justices' Manual with me to study in bed. For a time also, I was in charge of the two county courts and had to read the Annual County Courts Practice to keep abreast of the legal jargon. To add to my burden, because it was wartime, there were endless new government regulations out daily. It was quite a legalistic labyrinth. I still remember the first person we had to send to prison. I cried all night. He was an Irish tinker who had broken into the post office at Pencader for food. An unfortunate choice. The Postmaster, Mr Haydn Davies, was on the bench of magistrates. Poor Paddy did not have a fixed-abode address so had to be sent down.

I was really into a new world. Quite often I would have to attend the Assizes at Haverfordwest or Carmarthen. I guess I must have looked like a forlorn tree in the middle of the Sahara – the only woman amongst all the men. I remember the first Assizes I had to attend at Haverfordwest. I was very nervous. I dressed correctly in black and even wore a hat; a cute little one almost like a bowler, decorated with a bunch of violets in front. The judge was Justice Salmon. I had never seen him before. I was sitting, listening, and trying to look intelligent. I was getting uneasy because I thought he was staring at me. Was my protocol at fault? Eventually, when he beckoned me to approach him, I knew I was in trouble. I waited for the reprimand. He took his time and even gave me a smile. I could feel my red hair scorching my brain. He put out his hand to touch my hat and spoke softly: 'I have been wondering if they were real violets. Don't they make them true to life these days?' He sensed my nervousness and invited me to lunch. No wonder he had climbed the ladder to his high position. In no time at all, he had surreptitiously found out that it was my first Assizes and that I was new to the legal world and would have preferred to be driving an ambulance on the continent. Sadly, I never saw him again and although I wore my hat to all the other Assizes, hoping that another Judge perhaps might be curious about the violets, and take me to lunch, it never happened.

I don't know how we all survived the war years. There was such a lot to do. I could never be a nine-to-five career person.

Whatever court we had to attend, I used to start at 7am and quite often worked until 11 at night. There were so many summonses with so many new acts passed that the public was sometimes unaware that they were breaking the law. But it wasn't all hard labour. If there was a lull at times in the office, the boss and I would stir up a tumultuous debate. The topic might be arty – he was the nephew of Allen Raine, the novelist. He was also high church and our biblical fights were as noisy as a sea in storm. Quite often clients would have to wait until the turbulence abated.

Then, even after work, for me, there were village responsibilities.

Village Activities

Cenarth didn't have a village hall. In fact we still haven't got one. But we are very lucky for the last number of years that we have the Methodist chapel, with a good-sized vestry, opening its doors to all village activities. We even have a superior eisteddfod held there every year, with Elma, the wife of the Blue-Riband tenor Washington James, doing most of the arranging. It is so good to have 'Washie', such a celebrity, in our village.

During the war years, and for some time after, we had to use the church hall. And use it we did. Sometimes we had two or even three concerts in a week depending on how many of our servicemen and servicewomen were home on leave. There were about a dozen of our young people serving in the Army, Navy or Air Force. We lost only one: Ivor Rees. He was on the border of the boundary decided by the committee but had been adopted on our list.

Arranging the use of the church hall for each concert was almost a battle in itself. The vicar, a lovely old gentleman, over ninety years of age, was a born refuser. His stance was indisputable. The hall belonged to the church, and he visualised all the crowds gathering at the concerts desecrating his holy building. After a lengthy weighing of the pros and cons each time, he would eventually grant permission. I think he was the only person ever to escape seeing my red hair bursting into flames before his eyes.

He had a mischievous streak. too. He taught us an action song, the 'Keep Moving' one. We used to be invited to sing it at one or two concerts and it went somewhat like this:

> One finger, one thumb keep moving,
> Two fingers, two thumbs keep moving etc.
> One leg, one arm keep moving etc.

And then

Both arms, both legs keep moving . . .

and it ended with all of us falling on top of each other. The old
vicar's laughter was a joy to hear.

It was amazing the number of concerts we held week after
week. People were so generous with their time. I had a rota of
artistes at my beck and call – some local, some from all over
Pembrokeshire, Cardiganshire and Carmarthenshire. I couldn't
possibly list all the people who helped but one or two still stand
out in my memory. There was one faithful one throughout the
years. Captain Jack Johns, Cardigan – a wonderful bass-
baritone. A telephone call, even at the eleventh hour, would
secure his services. His repertoire was engaging and endless.
And one could never forget Madame Thomas, Newcastle
Emlyn. She deserved the honoured address. I never knew her
Christian name. She was such fun, if rather a hefty problem at
times. My car engine collapsed one night while taking her, and
five other artistes, home up the steep Bryndioddef hill in Adpar.
I was the 'Jack of all trades' at these Welcome Home concerts
and one duty was to collect and deliver home the artistes, who
were always giving their services free of charge. I guess I was
the only one in the village able to do so. Throughout the war
years I was given extra petrol coupons by an extremely
generous garage owner in Newcastle Emlyn. I knew him as
Ben, and to this day I haven't a clue why I was chosen as the
recipient of those priceless chits that kept my car on the road
during the whole time of such severe restrictions.

I suppose it was a very stressful time for all, but most of us
had so much to do, that we hardly noticed. It was blackout time
and there were no signposts, which for me, with no sense of
direction, added greatly to my confusion. I remember taking
back some artiste somewhere to the wilds of Pembrokeshire. At
well after 3am, I was still going round in circles at Rosebush,
continually returning to the same point!

This happened time after time for our artistes came from far and wide. There was J.S., for instance, who lived somewhere in the wilds around Brynberian, a tonic as a comic reciter in those dark days. We could always rely on the Cole Joneses, two sisters from Tegryn, who would lend a hand as accompanists. A more or less regular accompanist, also, was Lady Ann – Ann Weeks – from Newcastle Emlyn. The 'lady' we attached teasingly as she was so elegant and proper in every way. She was later appointed Mistress of the Robes for the Bardic Circle at the National Eisteddfod, a job she did exceedingly well. Also, if I remember rightly, we had young Joyce, the niece of Sally Jones, Tŷ'r Ddôl, helping out at the piano when necessary, though she was only nine or ten years old at the time.

Our faithful locals who had not been called up, farmers and what have you, were at every concert, boys like Charles Williams, Gobedig (baritone), and Marks James, Penfeidr (tenor), who would bring the house down each time with their rendering of the Gendarmes duet. And one could never forget Willie Cilfod (son of Philip John and Katie, my mother's friend). Willie was a tenor, our own Gigli. He had an astounding voice but had never had any training. I still, even today, feel very annoyed with myself that I did not record him singing at my home. I had a Grundig recorder, the only one in the village I think, but with all the activities of that period I missed out on a golden opportunity. His father, Philip John, had almost as good a voice. He had a very, very bad stammer and sometimes could only communicate by singing. He adored singing. Though not a chapelgoer, he never missed a chapel singing festival in all the years I knew him. He, and some of the men outside the village, would call at my home to sing hymns and I would have to accompany them on the piano generally until long after midnight.

I well remember one night when Philip John and five of his companions came in for their musical treat. They left about 1am. They were a cheerful crowd and the sing-song had gone well. I managed to jump into bed just before 2am. I was about to settle for some much needed sleep when I heard quite a commotion outside. I peeped through the upstairs window, and saw the departed group coming up the drive again. I put on a dressing gown and went to investigate. It seems they had walked about two miles to a crossroads when one of them reminded Philip John that he hadn't sung his favourite hymn that night, namely *Calon lân yn llawn daioni* ('A pure heart full of goodness'). After pawing the ground in frustration as he failed to get a word out, he finally sang his message in Welsh: 'Must go back, must go back . . . back.' And back they came. I sat at the piano dutifully. In the morning my mother and Aunty Hannah upstairs said they had never heard such inspirational singing. I am sure that even the singing of a Welsh rugby crowd in a Wales-against-England win, could not have been more heart-warming. I had to chuckle, though, at the lack of sleep that the group had to endure that night. Suffice it to say that no one would again remind Philip John that he had forgotten to sing his favourite hymn.

Musicians are sometimes a little egotistic. That can, admittedly, be forgiven if you are blessed with a good voice. Not all of us are, however. I could easily compare mine to a crow in the throes of influenza. Throughout the Welcome Home concerts, I would sometimes have to fill in the gaps with some calypso singing. One or two regulars would bring me some juicy village gossip and I would hurriedly write some verses and sing them. The voice didn't matter if the words were funny. My target as a rule would be Mrs Hannah Sexton, one of the most amiable persons in the village. But, like myself, she would run to act first and then stop to think: a recipe for mishaps that I could then exploit on stage! She really was a treasure, taking everything with a smile and always coming back for more. Her youngest daughter, Enid, married Primo, a very well-liked Italian ex-prisoner of war who had been posted to the Henllan Camp not far away. Sadly we have lost Primo but Enid and their son Richard still live in the village.

Looking back now at the concerts, they were cheerful events

considering we were all working at such speed, with plenty of laughs and inevitably some hiccups, too. And, if time allowed, I even squeezed in the odd play, a source of great mirth all round.

Of course, every member of the committee wanted to be in the cast and the theme would have to be worked around keeping everyone happy. The faithful audience along the years deserved a little variety. I can still remember two of the committee members who deserved an Oscar each for playing the same character for all those years. Marged Alltybwla, a great behind-the-scenes worker for each Welcome event, was too shy to have a speaking part so had to become a waitress. This she coped with superbly since her sister owned the Cawdor Hotel at Newcastle Emlyn. My big sister Get, too, was a very able committee worker but in no way a public speaker; too nervous to be a waitress, she had to be a non-gossiping postwoman. Both carried their labels with pride.

I think, however, that our over-enthusiasm might have dented the war effort on one occasion.

I had written a more superior than usual play, necessitating a young hero. Young men around at the time were as scarce as a trickle of water in a drought. But luck does wear a smile occasionally. Ken Jones, Parcybras – Private Ken Jones – was home on three weeks' leave, and was ideal for the part. We needed his presence more than his acting ability, so in he was roped! This was a very special one-off performance and our spies had found out that the well-known concert party Bois y Frenni, from the Preseli area, were going to be present. We had great respect for them and did not want to be caught napping. With spit and polish, everything was going well. The stage was set for the Saturday before Ken had to return to barracks the following week.

The Thursday before this momentous event, disaster struck. At the time, I'm ashamed to say, it almost amounted to the dropping of a bomb: Ken had received a curt and immediate call back. There was no way he could be replaced in the play in so short a space of time. And no way would we let Bois y Frenni take over our stage for the night. We started to contact people who could help to grant Ken two extra days – not a lot to ask. We tried our good friend, Captain Johns, who somehow at some time had been attached to Army headquarters somewhere. No joy there. Then we tried David Evans of Newcastle Emlyn, a top man with the British Legion. He suggested a Colonel Lloyd, I think, in Cardiff. In the end my rash red hair won. I found out that Ken was stationed in Catterick – a well-known landmark for Welsh people as it is mentioned in the oldest surviving Welsh poem, *Y Gododdin*, by Aneirin. I telephoned and demanded to talk to the general in charge of Ken's regiment. After cutting yards and yards, feet and feet, and then inches and inches of red tape, I at last spoke to this important commander. Actually I don't think I'd ever spoken to even a sergeant before, but my mission was important. Luckily common sense prevented me from blurting out that the favour I was asking was a life-and-death matter. Play-acting in wartime did not come into that category by any stretch of anybody's elastic. So I plastered him with all the Welshness I could muster about Catterick. How it was mentioned way back in the sixth century, and jabbered along also about Ken's home village of Cenarth and our Celtic origins. I think in desperation he finally got a word in and agreed that Ken would have special dispensation for this gala night providing he was back on duty two days after the event. Hallelujah! We were saved and gave the Pembrokeshire lads under their unique conductor, the gifted W.R. Evans (Wil Glynsaethman) of Mynachlog Ddu, our best shot. I confess, I did worry, though, after our play was critically acclaimed, that Ken might have been thrown into a glass house, which I had heard was an unhappy military punishment. But Ken was always adamant that he had received no punishment, only a little envy from his fellow soldiers.

One would have thought that quiet little Cenarth in the Teifi valley would have been immune from any knock-on effects of the Great War across the Channel. Not quite so. We certainly did not have the devastation of cities like Cardiff and Swansea, but we had a scare or two.

My first contact with the enemy was at Birmingham. My sister, whose work had taken her to Staffordshire, had fallen in love with Graham, the organist at the chapel in the village of Armitage. He had been called up and more than likely would be posted abroad, and they decided they would like to be married before that happened. So in 1940, I made my way to Armitage to be bridesmaid. In Birmingham I had to change at New Street for Snow Hill, or was it the other way round? The enemy was dive-bombing and I was literally dragged to a shelter by some Good Samaritan. The wedding went off well but I spent the night in an air-raid aid post with my sister's new sister-in-law, an air-raid warden. Between endless cups of tea and some spicy jokes from visiting villagers, I became very accustomed to the piercing noise of sirens.

I had taken a dislike to Birmingham, and it still clings. I decided to go back home through London. There again, I was physically assaulted for my own good. I was walking down Bond Street, a posh street at that time. But the enemy, indifferent to class, was at that moment trying to destroy it. I spent the night in an underground shelter. I was thankful to those people who hauled me to safety both times. The camaraderie during wartime is almost unbelievable. What a shame we cannot hang on to it in peacetime, too.

We settled down in the village to carry on our humble help to the war effort. But the unexpected was never far away. In fact around this time there were two very uneasy occurrences. On the first occasion we had a full house with visitors from Porthcawl, W.P. Thomas, an ocean colliery director and his elderly wife and two daughters, Dilys and Tegwen; my semi-invalid mother; widowed Aunty Hannah; my big sister Get and myself. Jimpy, our Welsh terrier, and Morgan the cat had to have bed and breakfast for the time being in the cottage down the garden. I had just been settling them for the night and was vaguely surprised that Jimpy, normally the best behaved of dogs, was rather nervous. I took it that he was sulking because of having to spend the night in the cottage. Before I managed to close the door, he pushed past me and ran furiously towards the house. I followed up the path. By then I could hear the rumbling of an aeroplane. I looked up at the sky and could see, quite a distance away, a kind of ball of fire in the sky. I immediately thought it was the Germans coming to bomb us. I raced to the house and ordered everybody out and up the drive to the main road. Get, Dilys and Teg guided the elders as if they had had professional training.

By now the threat was nearer and we could see it was a huge ball of fire heading for our house. I was on the telephone alerting the Police and Fire Brigade. Since I was working in police courts at that time, I was known to most of the officers. In the end the aeroplane came down in a quarry just across our Awmor stream in a field rented by us during the war. It was not, as I had feared, a German plane, but a British one that was in trouble and had lost its way. The superintendent in charge asked me if I would wait at the entrance to the field, and direct a lorry full of airmen who had been called from a dance in Cardigan, to the scene of the tragedy. I did. The lorry arrived and the men tumbled out. I can still, after all those years, hear one callous voice asking 'Where are the bloody stiffs?' Wars don't only kill, but destroy normal, decent souls, too.

Two men were saved, and four killed. The army took over for the following six weeks. The scattered corpses were brought for a while over to our garage. The two men who survived were brought to the house and we did what we could for them before they were taken to Cardigan hospital. Later the following morning, Dilys, Tegwen and I went to visit them but found that they had been spirited away and a wall of secrecy built around their new destination. I hear that they did come back to the village some years ago. Unfortunately I was in America at the time and did not know they had been invited. I would have liked to have talked to them again.

The Bretons

A second wartime occurrence proved, of necessity, a clandestine affair, unknown to the villagers. Again, the cottage down the garden, Y Gegin Fach ('The Little Kitchen') played a serious part in events. As I explained, I landed up working in police courts so was never called up, thus I had little knowledge of what was happening on the continent. Roy Evans, it seems, had assured the authorities that I was in a necessary job and could not be replaced. I naturally worried about Per – as a war correspondent, he was likely to be in the thick of the fighting – but tried to cheer myself up by hanging on to the old adage that 'no news is good news'.

It was very late on a dark night when I became alerted to a knock on the door. A rather weary looking friend of Per, whom I had met once or twice before, stood there. Under Per's instructions, he had smuggled himself across the channel. He assured me that so far Per was not in trouble, but several of his friends in Brittany were. The French were hounding all Breton nationalists – he himself had been branded a nationalist and was under sentence of death. Would it be possible, if they managed to reach Wales, to hide them before transferring them to Ireland?

Thus it came about that, at times, our Cegin Fach down the garden harboured sometimes one or two, and indeed at one time, five Breton nationalists, who were facing death because they wanted to be Breton and not French. I suppose it was a very difficult time for the French since the enemy was actually on their land. My family was not too happy but they knew of Per and that I had great faith in him. With the help of one or two trusted Welshmen, we ferried them at carefully appointed times to Ireland and safety. There was only one rule. They had, of course, to come under a feigned name and must never disclose to us their real names in case we inadvertently let slip. If the authorities ever found them, they would be returned to France and certain death.

In those days I was an idealist and had the pride of a Welsh nationalist so counted it more or less my duty to help our Breton cousins. How we got away with it has baffled me ever since. After all, we had policemen calling for a chat occasionally since I was working with them at the time. One of my greatest friends was Sylvan Howells, the editor of our local paper *The Cardigan and Tivy-side Advertiser* ('The Teifi-side' for short) and he also would call at the house every day to discuss all sorts of things. When I confessed to him, after the war, my help in these probably illegal, but hopefully humane, secret operations, I really had a serious telling-off for hiding from him his greatest ever wartime scoop!

Little did he know that there was another untold story that was too raw in the telling even to such a close friend. It still is. I scribbled off a poem on a scrap of paper a long time ago but cannot find it now. I can only recall a line or two, which is probably a blessing. Frustrations are not good fodder for creative thought.

> Wars do not only leave their dead,
> They leave broken hearts, the splinters
> too raw and bloody
> for even a super plastic surgeon
> to stick together and make whole . . .

A Breton friend on another dark night brought the news that Per was in prison and likely to be put to death. He had been reported for collaborating with a German soldier. Otto, his good friend when working on a paper in Berlin, was in the German army in France. They met, and of course, as old friends, talked. Per was reported and immediately stuck in prison. His life was in danger. Could he be saved by coming to Wales? There was, of course, no doubt. There were plenty of good friends in Brittany to help. I immediately started planning. Oddly, one person came to mind instantly. I had heard that Piaf was doing a wonderful job with the resistance movement. I guess one only knows one's strength when faced with a crisis. With the help of this incredible friend who had access to men who had the technical know-how of getting people in and out of a country ravaged with war, we snatched Per out of prison and with unbelievable optimism, faith and stubbornness got him to the haven of our Welsh Gegin Fach.

A friend's van took him to the crossing to Ireland. He was determined to find Otto and be cleared of being a collaborator before making himself known in Wales. But there were clouds of complications. It took years. Finally he got help to go to the United States. Eventually he traced Otto and everything looked hopeful.

Per had, however, been abused in prison and knew that he would have to have an operation to relieve the pressure in his head. It was an operation that he would not survive.

There was nothing left but an emptiness that even the precious gems of memories could never hope to fill.

The Breton connection, though, did not end there. One afternoon the Rev. Ben Owen and the Rev. Lewis Valentine called at my home. I had known Ben Owen for some time and, of course, knew of Lewis Valentine, both ardent Welsh nationalists. I had great admiration for both. We discussed the unfairness of the French government labelling all nationalists as collaborators and, without a shred of evidence of any wrongdoing, issuing sentences of death against them. It became clear that there were two in Wales at the moment. They had escaped under false names and were being helped by Mr Gwynfor Evans at his home in Llangadog. He hadn't room for them permanently and was looking for a safe place for them to stay. Because I knew that three Breton nationalists had been executed by the French Government, it was a strict rule at home that we never discussed Bretons, even with other Bretons, as things were so unstable in France that even an innocent word might cost a life. I don't know whether Ben Owen, who was well known in the district, had somehow sniffed a rumour of the ships that passed in the night to Ireland from the Gegin Fach, but he was a persuasive charmer and when the two Reverends left, I had agreed that if the family concurred, we would take the two Bretons into our home. There was no fear the family would let Per down.

The two Bretons arrived and became Albert and Robert to the villagers. Both were lovers of their country, and one was on the list of collaborators and under sentence of death, probably because he happened to be an international lawyer and had been partly educated in Germany. Robert stayed for a little over two years, I think, and Albert for five or six years. Albert became known to a lot of well-known people in Wales and became a fine artist and potter. I took up serious oil painting at that time, too and almost became a second Grandma Moses who, starting at eighty years of age, became a much acclaimed artist throughout the world.

We were very, very careful not to draw attention to outsiders. We were nearly caught out once, though. With the help of one or two trusted friends, we were sending pamphlets to be distributed over Brittany to let the Breton people know how the Bretons were misjudged by the French. The Gegin Fach again became part of the plan. I had a typewriter and typed them there before they were printed by a trusted friend. There was another Breton friend of Albert's, having been befriended if I remember rightly, by Swansea University. He was known as Dr Moger, and, under his true name, was a very successful publisher in Paris. He decided one day to come down to see Albert at my home. Whether he became a little too bold, or a little too careless, he was followed down by a reporter from the London Magazine *Time and Tide*. Luckily Cenarth is a small place and in those days we knew everyone in the village. A stranger was held to be a suspect until proven otherwise. We sent our spy to the village pub where he found a man asking a lot of unusual questions. Albert became a prisoner in his own room at my home Glanawmor and Dr Moger was dispatched to a friend in Pembrokeshire until the London man had lost scent of the trail to the Gegin Fach. We knew we had been lucky and because we thought the risk might have been severe, we brought our pamphleteering to a sudden end.

I had one more small tussle with the French authorites. We had a Breton friend, Jacques, who acted for his fellow Bretons in prison for their love of Brittany, and was himself in prison because he had taken up their legal grievances. He had developed heart trouble and his friends worried for his life if he was kept locked up without medical treatment. There were prominent and respected people in Wales, like Cynan, Euros Bowen and his brother, Geraint, the Rev. Dyfnallt Owen and others, trying their utmost to get him released. He was due to appear in court and that, everyone feared, would further prolong his time without treatment. As usual when I was frustrated, my red-hair genes would commandeer my common sense. With sheer recklessness, I cabled the judge sitting on the case with a heart-breaking sob story. It happened to be more or less true, because Jacques's wife, Elizabeth, was bordering on a breakdown. When I confessed to this later, the ones who knew more about the French system than I did, thought I had done more harm than good, as the Welsh and the French have different temperaments. I agreed. But, suddenly, Jacques was freed. I take no credit for that, but am only thankful that for once, the French faced up to their mistake of locking him up in the first place.

And that reminds me of the time I found myself locked up in France. Not that pleasant – even though at the time, my aversion to such things was not as cemented as it is today. I do admit, however, that this hiccup was partly of my own making.

I've already more than hinted at my involvement with the Bretons. One really nice gentleman, we called him Joseph, I think, had been staying at my home a few times. He was the liaison officer between France and Brittany, and he and Albert, who was still with us, were good friends. He telephoned one day. There was a conference in Versailles of *Les Minorites* – the

95

'little' countries like Wales and Catalonia, and those of Eastern Europe. He wanted me to be there to represent Wales.

I said I didn't think it was possible. I would have to leave in a little over half an hour to get to London for the night and then catch a boat to Calais the next morning. In any case, I wouldn't be much use in their conference as I hadn't been taking my usual interest in what was happening in these small countries recently. But Albert, the Breton, could be persuasive. He reeled it all off. He ordered me to go and dress; my big sister Get would pack for me, and he had a bundle of papers to go in my luggage that I could read on the way there and know everything that would be needed at the conference. Get and Albert were working like robots so I had no one to defend me. I went to dress.

I had a wonderful night in London. A doctor friend wined and dined me and in the morning I was away to catch my boat to arrive at the conference hotel in Versailles. My sudden outing was turning out to be interesting. When we were passing through to board, they were checking handbags as there was a strict restriction on the amount of money we could take out of the country because someone had been caught taking a lot more than the specific amount allowed, which I think was £25. I never have a lot of money so I knew I was quite safe. My worry was the thought of the officer seeing the inside of my bag – absolutely worse than an unmade bed. I could see the man floundering through my untidy mess, rustling up a £1 note here and a ten shilling note there

He actually found much more than I had bargained for. In fact, it was fast becoming double what I was allowed. I stood very embarrassed; I did not know I had that much money. The man was glaring and spat 'I'll have to search your luggage'.

When he saw the huge bundle of newspapers that Albert had planted in my case to ease my ignorance, I knew by one glance at my inquisitor's rigid jaw-line that he thought he had found a wicked fraudster. My face became redder than my hair. My eyes became glued to my feet in shame. He was on the money hunt of his career. I couldn't look but knew that he was meticulously going through every corner of each copy. I would miss my boat and pondered whether they would put me in prison in England or France. I was about to go on my knees to beg him to let it please be England when I heard a huge chuckle. I looked up in surprise. The tormentor was laughing and saying, 'I can quite believe that you didn't know how much money you were carrying if you can take this with you to the continent.' Still struggling with laughter he was holding up a very, very fat West Wales Telephone Directory. I worked it out quickly. Albert had picked up the bundle of papers without noticing the wayward extra passenger.

The official had had his fun and probably being sorry for me did not confiscate my extra money. I smiled and thanked him sweetly, adding ' I love reading telephone directories.'

That flippant face-saving rebounded on me. I was about to experience an uncomfortable setback. In the evening at the conference hotel at Versailles, the delegates met and arranged a party to tour the palace. Apart from myself, there was only one other delegate from Britain at the conference, a Professor David Shillan from London, a bearded Russian lookalike. I dislike touring with a party as I am apt to absent-mindedly wander, but David Shillan, thinking he ought no doubt to pay attention to his fellow Britisher, entreated me to join. Not wanting to appear stand-offish, I did.

We had a lady guide and we moved from room to room with no mishaps. We came to Marie Antoinette's room. Now my interest ballooned. Marie had been on my mind for years. I had even written a play about her so I was determined to inspect even the molecules of dust in her room. The party was urged to move on by the guide, but I wasn't ready to go and knew that I could catch up with them. I turned the bed-cover over and looked under the bed. Finally I was satisfied and went to catch up with the others. The door was locked. I struggled and struggled with no luck. I was locked in. I shouted and then yelled in all the languages I knew – even added some non-dictionary words too by the end! By now the lights were turned off and it was absolutely dark. I tried to take a rest on the edge of Marie's bed but her head kept rolling under my feet. At the crack of dawn, I thought I heard a cockerel crow three times but that I am convinced was my confused mind.

It was well after 5am when I heard the rustling of keys. Joseph and the Professor had finally missed me and worked out that I had last been seen at the palace. It turned out that we had been the last guided tour that night and the guide had been locking doors as she went along. I never did blame Marie Antoinette. It was the blackness that got me – I could do nothing but treble count my sins all night. I did go back on my own another time and made peace with my conscience.

I loved France, and especially Paris with its magical excitement when I was young. Now when I go, I make straight for the Père la Chaise cemetery to pay my respects and give thanks at the tomb of Edith Piaf, for having known and been accepted as a friend by the little sparrow, my *Llwyd Bach y Baw*.

The second war to end all wars did end. But it did take a very long time for me to convince Mr Roy Evans that it had finally done so. Eventually I got free and set about returning to London to re-mould my writing career. In a way I had been lucky. Being in police courts had shown me life in almost all its aspects and had given me confidence that I could be a better writer.

Things at home were fairly stable. My mother was holding her own against the Parkinson's. Aunty Hannah was with us permanently, and Big Sister Get was, as usual, in complete control, with the help of Emma, from the village, and Dolly from Aberporth who came in to work for us. Later, I would probably be more needed at home. For the moment it was the magic of London, with frequent visits home at weekends, and the dreams of becoming a full-time writer. But, as usual, my topsy-turvy gene came to life one weekend and changed all that.

Dewi Emrys

When I came home to Wales at the first rumblings of war, Dewi Emrys left London, too, and settled in Cardiganshire at Y Bwthyn, Talgarreg, where he remained for the rest of his life. He kept in touch and would appear on our doorstep from time to time with the same greeting 'I'm starving, Luned'. Sometimes that was literally true.

Dewi Emrys had absolutely no financial sense. But he would brag that he had a millionaire cousin, Sir David James, Sutton Hall, who had made his money mostly in London cinemas. Dewi would be proud to tell the world that his cousin would send him periodic cheques.

The only virtue, I think, in having red hair was that none of my disagreements with people was ever long-standing. It was a sudden blazing furnace, too sudden often I admit, but once the battle was over, the truce was a lasting one. My conflict with Sir David James was, however, more protracted; the longest I ever had, in fact. It was finally over Dewi Emrys's Memorial in Pwllderi.

It was quite true that Sir David would send his cousin a cheque occasionally. I remember once having a call for help from the poet: there was no food in his cupboard. I understood he'd been probably working on a poem and had forgotten that even a genius must eat. I went up to Talgarreg with provisions. The following night I called at the Bwthyn to see if he was alright. I was so relieved; he looked so pleased with himself. He'd had a cheque for fifteen guineas from his cousin. I was about to tell him I was so glad and that he'd be alright then for a couple of days, when, with a roguish look, he beckoned me to follow him to the back of the cottage. With the delight of a toddler on Christmas Day, he showed me a brand new fishing rod. 'Went to Aberystwyth this morning and bought it. It was exactly 15 guineas.' How could one erase the joy of an innocent boy?

Another time he'd had eighteen guineas and called me up to see what he'd bought: a new dance dress for his daughter Dwynwen. There was no point in trying to get Dewi to change his way of life. I was really uneasy at times about him. I wasn't always around to see that he had food in the house. The neighbours were all kind but we all had our own lives to attend to, so I wrote to Sir David James, a few times actually. I explained that, since his creative cousin was not spending the money on food, it might be a better idea for Sir David, with all his much-vaunted financial acumen, to stop sending cheques directly to the Bwthyn, and to arrange with the village store that there was always enough food in the house to keep Dewi Emrys healthy. I never got a response.

When we were arranging the poet's memorial, and accepting donations from his numerous friends, I received a cheque for £500 from Sir David James. I sent it back with a polite note saying that his cousin had really needed that generous sum to help him stay alive. The cheque was returned. I sent it back. I received it back again. After the third coming and going, our chairman, the admirable Councillor Glyn Davies, O.B.E., Aberarth, decided we had better accept it, adding that probably the great entrepreneur only understood how to deal with money and not the necessities of life. I forgave Sir David and sent him a polite thank you and a copy of our gala commemorative service leaflet.

Yes, money to Dewi Emrys was an irrelevant, and often non-existent, commodity. The Wayfarers (more of whom later) were once on an outing to Saint Fagans, Cardiff. Everything had been arranged and we had all dined sumptuously in a first-rate hotel – all of us except our chief, Dewi Emrys. We failed to coax him to the table, which was very unusual for one who loved his food.

We respected his wishes, however, and, at his request, travelled home through the town of Bridgend. We all nodded acceptance of this. The place naturally had fond memories. He had won his fourth National Eisteddfod Chair there in 1948. He had cause to feel proud. As we came up to the biggish hotel in Bridgend, there was a command to halt. The coach driver obliged and pulled in to park. This was where the poet had had a wonderful meal to celebrate his win in 1948. He knew the manageress and would dine there. He invited me to be his guest. I pointed out that we had all eaten but to no avail. He and I went in.

The manageress did remember him and gave him a royal welcome. Dewi was king and ordered according to status. I could only pretend to eat and did not want to spoil the joyous atmosphere. After he had finished his pudding, which had taken him almost ten minutes to select, he turned to me like a lost child and asked simply, 'Luned. Have you got money to pay?' Luckily, I had. Some of our members thought it was a con trick. I don't think so. He merely wanted me to share his proud moment and that to him, was way above the value of money. My red hair remained calm, but had anyone else invited me to dinner and then expected me to pay, the burning flames around my head would have been comparable to those in the nether regions portrayed by the old visiting preachers at my Bryn Seion when I was young.

But what of these Wayfarers – or *Fforddolion Ceredigion*, to give the society its birthname.

Dewi Emrys, home from London since the beginning of the war, was sitting in the Brynhoffnant Inn, near Synod Inn one day, feeling pretty lost, I imagine, after the hurly-burly of Fleet Street life. The landlord was a devoted friend, Dai Lloyd Jones, a humorist and man of considerable culture. All around him were rural characters discussing poetry, music and all sorts of country activities. Dewi Emrys was notable for his love of companionship. He was fascinated by the intellect of the

101

ordinary people around him. Thus was born the society, Cymdeithas Fforddolion Ceredigion ('The Cardiganshire Wayfarers' Society'), whose aims were, in his own words (or, at least, my translation of them)

1 To gather together intelligent and seemly adults yearning to restore the old evening companionship that was so typical of rural countryside before foreign influences destroyed the old home industries, leaving a huge void where once a vast population thrived, and the silence of ruins, instead of pride of craftsmanship and the dignity of a nation's culture.

2 To invite men and women of standing to speak on subjects close to Welsh hearts, and arrange debates, talks and free discussions amongst the members themselves.

I can remember many happy and truly inspiring meetings; I can remember one or two stormy ones, too. Sometimes our best intentions were floored. For example, I remember when John Griffiths, BBC producer, had invited me to send in a script in Welsh on the Fforddolion Society. I must admit, Dewi Emrys could be difficult to handle at times, so I had agreed at John's request to have a rehearsal at Brynhoffnant Inn before the live broadcast at Swansea Studios. I had composed words, on a familiar Welsh air, as a chorus for the Fforddolion. Dewi asked my permission to alter one word in one verse in order to improve the song. I consented immediately; I would have agreed to alter the whole composition if our top bard had suggested it. But when it came to singing the chorus, the new word apparently did not fit as well as the original one. Eser Evans, one of our leading members and a noted musician, said bluntly, that it caused a counter-accent. Dewi Emrys jumped on him: 'Who are you, a snippet of a surveyor, to tell me, Dewi Emrys, that the word has a counter-accent.' The surveyor, of course, stood up to defend himself, but Dewi insisted that Eser had no right to a different opinion.

Of course, I marched right in telling Dewi Emrys that everyone had the right to a personal opinion. The literary lion turned on me: 'You are nothing but a parrot to Eser.' By now I could feel my hair flamenco dancing. I demanded an apology. Oddly enough, this runaway battle was fought through the medium of English. For some reason or another, I never can fight verbally except in English. By this time each temper was as obstinate as the other. I could see Dewi's nose extending by inches as he spat out 'I won't take part in this broadcast'. Even though I knew I was doing injustice to the script, the producer and certainly to the listeners, I accepted his withdrawal and handed him his overcoat politely and helped him to put it on.

The other Wayfarers were wiser than I was. Sam James, the Glanrhyd schoolmaster on one side, and the genial landlord Dai Lloyd Jones, on the other, were trying their utmost to get me to prevent Dewi from leaving the room. But I had had a bellyful of trying to rein in a genius, and was far from being helpful. I knew full well that the following day there would be a broacasting gap that could not possibly be filled adequately. But this was the night of the battle. I let him go.

In spite of his egotism and belief in the infallibility of his work, underneath Dewi Emrys had a gracious nature. Before he reached the door, he took a step or two back and offered his hand across the table to me: ' I'm apologising, Luned.' We shook hands and I said 'Let's get on with the rehearsal.' The storm passed and peace reigned.

After that quivering night, I had no more trouble with Dewi Emrys. I still had to stand in for John Griffiths at rehearsals, and I included the bard in as many of my programmes as possible, mainly because he was an asset, but also I knew he needed the money. Indeed, after the Battle of Brynhoffnant, instead of arguing over a point, or instead of cracking the whip which no doubt was sometimes justified, he would actually ask my view on the matter. He would also ask Eser's advice on all things musical. Yes. Beneath the *Fi Fawr* that he probably used as a guard to defend himself from the many attacks on his way of life, he had a modest, gentlemanly nature.

Including Dewi Emrys in a programme was as good as any slimming recipe. I swear I used to shed pounds at each programme. We had to start for the Swansea studios at least two or three hours before time to collect our most famous contributor. We would arrive at his cottage, *Y Bwthyn*, and, even if, by some stroke of luck, he was fully dressed, there would probably be at least one part of his face still unshaved. He complained that people were always accusing him of getting up late but nobody ever asked him what time he had gone to bed. (I sympathised. I am also a night owl!) On these outings we never got back the same day. After the broadcast, there would be post mortems, and one or two meals. Then, if we were lucky on our way home, we'd arrive at Porth-y-rhyd, a few miles from Carmarthen, at about 2am for the last meal of the night, or the first of the morning, rather! This was a ritual. After a royal welcome, we'd end up having beetroot sandwiches and pancakes. Then Dewi Emrys would take over and regale all aboard with his innumerable stories.

Even at a studio broadcast, which were all live in those days, there could be embarrassing moments. I remember once Dewi Emrys had a fairly lengthy speech to deliver. He went at it with gusto, closing his eyes and wandering away from the microphone, probably forgetting he was not on stage. I went quietly to grab his sleeve to ease him back to the microphone and all the listeners heard in the middle of his speech was 'Luned, what are you doing to me?' It took me a long time to get over that – I was even stopped by people in the street, asking me seriously to tell them what I had been doing to the poor fellow.

There was another heart stopper, too. It was a fishing programme for the BBC, with John Griffiths producing, and Aunty Hannah starring. Though she could be a handful sometimes, Dewi Emrys himself was far more problematic. At tea before the transmission, the great man gave us some sparkling fishing facts. John was impressed and asked me whether we could fit them into the script. I had no objection, but warned the producer that, knowing Dewi Emrys, we might not get the same spiel on transmission. Indeed, since there were others taking part, it might become a bit of a jumble.

In the end both John and I decided it was worth the risk. We went on air, but when it came to Dewi, we never got a repeat of the tea-time treats. It was a disjointed performance. In the end John had to come from behind his glass partition and join me at the microphone, and we had to ad lib until we could get back to the cues for the others taking part in the script. Still with Dewi Emrys, it was always a risk worth taking.

One of the Wayfarers' most pleasurable outings was the annual pilgrimage to Pwllderi in north Pembrokeshire, the area where the poet had spent his childhood; the area that had inspired his classic dialect poem *Pwllderi*. I shall never forget the first pilgrimage, sitting with him on the very boulder where he had originally composed it, and listening to him reciting his epic.

I remember writing him a poem that day. He was forever urging me to send him poems to include in his 'Poetry Corner' in the Welsh newspaper, *Y Cymro*. He was also constantly commanding me to compete at the National Eisteddfod. I guess competing was in his blood, but I never did find time to follow suit when he was alive. But this day at Pwllderi, I wrote him a verse or two. I think he sent it into the *Cymro*, more than once. I can only remember the first two lines:

> Safai yn gawr uwchben mawredd y creigiau,
> a'r byd wrth ei draed . . .

> ('He stood a giant above the majesty of the rocks,
> the world at his feet . . .')

We always ended these pilgrimages dining at Pwll Gwaelod, another divine spot not far away. Then in the early hours of the morning, Dewi Emrys, with a glass of crème de menthe in his hand, would recite *Pwllderi* with dramatic effect. We would end hours later, with his innumerable stories riding high on the crest of the waves. He should have been an actor. I have no doubt that he would have been another Richard Burton and would have walked the red carpet at Oscar time, a conquering hero.

Yes, as he ends his poem,

> A thina'r meddilie sy'n dwad ichi
> Pan foch chi'n ishte uwchben Pwllderi.
>
> ('Those are the thoughts that come to you
> As you sit above Pwllderi.')

They are our thoughts, too, as we turn to his memorial and have an endearing smile as we look at the two extra years of life that we somehow managed to have carved on his stone as if by an immortal hand!

But before leaving the Wayfarers, I must quote to you one of Dewi Emrys's many impressive pronouncements at our dinners. We were at the Poppit Hotel, St Dogmaels, enjoying a Welsh cultural evening as usual. There was another group, English speakers from the RAF station at Aberporth, sitting not far away. When we sang our national anthem in Welsh they began interrupting. Dewi Emrys asked them very politely to tone down the noise. One immediately became aggressive, belittling the Welsh and pointing out that Wales really had nobody to compare to their Shakespeare. Without raising his voice, but with clear diction, our Bard answered: 'You are right my friend. God in his mercy gave Shakespeare to England to relieve the flatness of the English mind.' Thereafter we were allowed absolute peace.

Dewi Emrys was in and out of my life in various ways until his death in 1952. And for some time after, actually. I became his biographer. I was ordered by him to become his biographer. And, in a weak moment, I agreed. We were at my old home then and we had had friends visiting. We also had Cynan, the only person to have been elected Archdruid of the Bardic Circle twice, and he had been entertaining us with a talk about his experiences. It had been a night to remember.

After the feast had ended and most of the guests had departed, Dewi as usual was again starving, so in the early hours, Dewi, a well-known barrister from Cardiff, an artist from Paris and I went and raided the pantry. Then, comfortably satisfied, Dewi Emrys took centre stage.

I do not know why he decided that night to unburden his whole life to us. Maybe he sensed that the end was not far away. Within a year we had lost this remarkable character.

The stars had gone to sleep and the dawn was exposing our tired faces as we listened. We knew that this was the confession of a soul. It was exhilarating, it was sad, and wholly embracing.

In the morning when he had finally covered the ups and downs of his life, he turned to me with renewed energy and gave his orders: a memorial stone at Pwllderi; a plaque at his final residence, Y Bwthyn. I guess he was a collector of plaques, he even suggested one at my home, Glanawmor, to let people know that he had stayed there. I pointed out to him that in later years we meant to build a bungalow across the road. Immediately he told me I should call my new home Glyn-y-Mêl. Then he recited a poem he had written to a Glyn-y-Mêl at Fishguard:

> There are elves to blue bells clinging,
> > down in Glyn-y-Mêl . . .
> Censers pearled with dew are swinging
> > down in Glyn-y-Mêl.
> Where the river foams and glitters,
> The first swallow always twitters
> > down in Glyn-y-Mêl.

I don't remember the rest at the moment. He included it in his *Rhymes of the Road*, published in 1928.

Years and years after,when we did build our bungalow in the 1980s, we called it affectionately 'Glyn-y-Mêl'. Before that I had used it as my nom de plume when I sent my poem 'Corlannau' to the National Eisteddfod at Bala, where I won my first National Crown in 1967. I am sure that our old friend would have appreciated that.

But back to that morning of the confessions when he ordered me to be his biographer. There was no way I could refuse, of course. And there was no way later that I could break a solemn promise, even when I realised that chasing and catching such a shooting star would land me with a migraine – even though I had never suffered a headache in my life. Eventually, with the help of a grant from the Arts Council, I stayed at home long enough for the reliable Gomerian Press (now Gomer), Llandysul, to publish in 1971 my best attempt at recording the ebbs and flows of a complex character. *Dyna'r meddilie sy'n dwad*. And what thoughts!

When Dewi Emrys died in 1952, rainbows faded. We had lost a colourful character. Certainly the eisteddfodic scene in Wales became duller and more staid. In our village Dewi Emrys would have been known as 'Dewi'r Llwy Bren' ('Dewi of the Wooden Spoon'). That was the nickname given to those apt to stir up and perpetuate controversy. Oh yes, our Dewi was a stirrer par excellence. He was a talented and dangerous competitor, mainly in the strict-metre poetry competitions and perfectly entitled to submit an entry each year, which he did. After winning his fourth National Bardic Chair in 1948, the Eisteddfod barons had had enough. I guess they wanted to appear politically correct even in those days. Dewi Emrys had to be stopped. But how? His poetry was still the best. So the academics became legal lions, and there was born a strict rule: no competitor was allowed to win one of the festival's major prizes more than twice. That is why, when I won my second National Crown, I became redundant.

On those occasions that Dewi Emrys did not win, he would never, like most of us, go home quietly to lick his wounds and hope for a better bunch of adjudicators the next time. Oh, no. He would declare a battle, if not a protracted war. Attacks and counter-attacks would deluge newspapers, local and otherwise, for weeks, and the rancour, sometimes personal, would fester for years. It was a good thing I suppose that we were not glued to the American way of life in those days, otherwise competitors of Dewi Emrys's calibre and those presumptious adjudicators would spend whole chunks of their lives battling their differences in law courts – or on daytime TV programmes!

Most people who knew Dewi Emrys would, I think, agree that he was his own worst enemy. Lots of people, because of his down-and-out way of life, labelled him an alcoholic. In all the years I knew him, he was definitely not so. Given a glass of crème de menthe in his hand, he would happily regale his listeners into the early hours and beyond. But that was born of his great need for jovial company.

I remember a story he once told us. He and another traveller were passing through Exeter on their way to Wales on a Saturday night, as Dewi was preaching at a Welsh chapel in the Rhondda valley on the Sunday. Neither had money, so Dewi suggested they should sing Welsh songs hoping that the Exeter Welsh would give them money, if not a bed for the night. They did collect four pounds, six shillings and seven pence and were lucky enough to be found by a police officer from Sir Fôn (Anglesey) who offered them a bed each in a cell for the night. They accepted and split the money between them.

Dewi Emrys put his precious two pounds, three shillings and three pence ha'penny safely in one of his boots and being in a policeman's house, put his boots outside the cell door. In the morning there was no trace of his boots or of his travelling companion. But Anglesey men are always generous. The policeman not only gave Dewi an old pair of boots but found him a lift to the chapel where he was to preach that morning.

Dewi Emrys was renowned as a powerful preacher and the chapel was more than packed when he arrived. Unfortunately, the policeman's feet and Dewi's did not twin easily. Dewi's walk into the chapel was anything but steady and stately. Hands went up half-covering mouths. The tittering turned to protest. The pure of heart, and most of them honestly thought they were, would not demean their holy thoughts with a drunk's sermon. One, head held high, reached the open door and marched out. Two more followed and then a stream. Dewi Emrys raised his eyebrows. He was a quick thinker. He discarded the pulpit and came to stand at the open door and recited a psalm. The nearest eased themselves back guiltily to their pews. Those who had slipped further away heard the proud voice and returned hastily to the fold. He was invited again to be their guest preacher in three months' time. I suspect all the sanctimonious Thomases were there as were many more. This, like many of the other wild stories about our poet, was a true one. In later years, my Uncle Griff confirmed it. He had been there and had travelled miles that Sunday morning to hear the much acclaimed genius.

I think most of us who knew Dewi Emrys will agree that his way of life caused many of his contemporaries to draw the wrong conclusions about him. I have always stuck by my mother's urging that one should know a person's circumstances before passing judgement. Or, as the man himself poetically put it (and I less poetically in its translation):

> Hawdd i wlad yw beirniadu – ar wen gaer
>   Hen gwch a fo'n mallu;
>   Aed ei feirniad i'w farnu
>   Draw i fôr y brwydro a fu.

> (It is easy for a nation to criticise – on a beautiful harbour
>   an old dilapidated boat;
>   Let those sitting in judgement
>   go out to the battling sea where the wreckage occurred.)

There is much, much more to this likeable mixed-up character. He left a rich legacy and to my mind has never been fairly honoured. He was a revered writer in Welsh and English; published volumes of poetry; was a very able tutor, holding classes under the auspices of the University of Wales over a wide area; his book on strict-metre poetry was a boon to many young, aspiring poets. His *Y Babell Awen* ('The Muse's Tent') column in *Y Cymro*, to which budding poets sent their work in order to benefit from Dewi Emrys's criticism, was probably his richest contribution to Wales, however. Many, many poets of today are thankful for his help and advice. Well, maybe I should subtract one or two from the 'many, many'. Our bard did not suffer fools gladly and his sting could be as sudden and perilous as a snake bite. I must confess in lashing out he combined the venom and vitriol of today's Anne Robinson and Simon Cowell. Pity he was born too soon to be rewarded, like them, financially.

He could be a wily wag at times. He desperately wanted to be noticed in Fleet Street. He had some articles, entitled 'Fishing Basket' to offer. He failed, however, to get an interview with G.K. Chesterton, a top Fleet Street man at the time. Having a great opinion of his own work, he slyly left his 'Fishing Basket' on the great man's desk. Chesterton found it, was curious and read the work. In a fluster he sent out his underlings to scour the Street for the author. The 'Fishing Basket' subsequently became a series of widely-read articles.

Yes, there are thoughts and thoughts. But I must move on.

Waldo

Sorry. I really meant to dump the poets and let you breathe again. But I've just remembered that someone asked me once who was my favourite poet and why. I found it a bit of a problem – the 'why' part, that is. There were two names, of course, that kept springing to mind, those of Dafydd ap Gwilym and Waldo. I still don't quite know why these two remain important. I have been trying to balance the answer Shylock's way.

Dafydd ap Gwilym has walked with me like a shadow since those young days of reciting psalms at our chapel singing-festivals when I was introduced to this bizarre fourteenth-century poet by the unassuming printer, David Richard Davies. As soon as I found the joy of the clicking consonants of his strict metre, I would find turning to Dafydd ap's poems warm and friendly, although I suppose half the time their meaning became my own suppositions. Later I adored Dewi Emrys's descriptive poem to Dafydd ap Gwilym. In fact, I often thought that my friend Dewi would have made a wonderful troubadour and had, sadly, once again, missed out on the most appropriate time and place of birth. Still, my idolisation of Dafydd ap might have become boring in the end, since I only seemed to get that warmth and difficult-to-describe stirring by turning to Dafydd ap Gwilym when I was in a cheerful mood. Surely poets are there for all moods?

Fate is kind to the genuinely ignorant, for I was later to meet that wonder-poet-for-all-moods, Waldo Williams. Well, I didn't actually meet him in person then. I got involved with his book of poems *Dail Pren* ('Tree Leaves'). I think it was Euros Bowen who aptly pointed out that the *pren* (tree) was the Muse or Inspiration (*Awen*) and the *dail* (leaves) the poems.

What a gem of a book! I browsed and browsed through it. Didn't understand a lot of the poems at first but found that if I was in a joyous mood, I would turn to *Dail Pren*. If I was in a sad, sad mood, I would also turn to *Dail Pren*. I decided that I had found my all-time favourite poet – Waldo – inspired by *hud a lledrith Sir Benfro* ('the enchantment of Pembrokeshire').

I think I felt a kind of affinity with the poet the first time I read *Dail Pren;* an at-homeness, if such a word exists. Two lines glued themselves to me and have stayed with me along the years.

> I'w phyrth deuai'r trafferthus
> A gwyddai'r llesg ddor ei llys

> (To her porch came the troubled souls,
> the feeble knew the door to her palace)

I don't quite remember now which poem I'm quoting from (and I'll lose my train of thought if I stop to look it up) but I do know that, then and now, Waldo describing his mother was also describing my grandmother. I found it again in that great poem of his *Y Tangnefeddwyr*:

> Chwiliai 'mam am air o blaid
> Pechaduriaid mwya'r lle.
> Gwyn eu byd tu hwnt i glyw,
> Tangnefeddwyr, plant i Dduw.

> (My mother would seek a word in favour
> of the greatest sinners in any place
> Blessed are they beyond hearing,
> Peacemakers, children of God)

I must apologise to the late Waldo and to any readers for attempting to translate the poet's work. It is far beyond my ability. Not only was he a great academic genius, he could turn our simple everyday words into irresistible pearls that clung to your sub-conscience. I find it very difficult, for instance, to translate the glorious word *Tangnefeddwyr*. 'Peacemakers' doesn't give me the lasting thrill that hearing the Welsh word can give me. It is like that word *hiraeth*. I know it is usually translated to 'longing', but, believe me, it never has the original's deep resonances; that profundity that brings me close to tears.

Waldo, when I did eventually meet him, had that unique child/man character that is so rare. He could be serious and funny almost in the same breath. I remember meeting him once on the National Eisteddfod field. It must have been the Port Talbot and District one since I was staying at the then Grand Hotel. On the *Maes* ('field') the rain was bucketing down as usual. I felt half drowned before Waldo caught up with me. He was looking for his friend, T. Llew Jones. By the time he had finished telling me in every minute detail how he was late arriving because of his valiant effort to iron his shirt properly for our foremost festival, I was in a state to send for a helicopter or a boat or whatever is needed to save a drowning person. Dripping, with premonitions of at least treble pneumonia, and offering a teaholic prayer for a cuppa, I suggested going back to the Grand Hotel, hoping that we would find (or at least, find somebody who could point him in the direction of) the Prifardd Llew. (*Prifardd* is the title bestowed on winners of the Chair and Crown competitions at the National Eisteddfod.) We did find the missing bard there, happily dry and enjoying himself. I made a run for an indoor (and heated) shower!

Another time I met Waldo, nothing went according to plan. I had Albert and Robert, the two Bretons, staying with me. They had heard of Waldo and were keen to meet him. As were a few more of my friends. So Waldo was invited to my home in Cenarth. Gracious, and anxious as usual to oblige, he arrived in the afternoon. We were quite a group and the anticipation of Waldo giving a talk was electric. I sat him in an easy chair with a cup of tea. He stared at us without saying a word for quite a while, then turned himself more comfortably in his chair and slept for over three hours.

We did get our talk, however. And I don't think any of us ever forgot it. Then after food and pleasantries, the outsiders left one by one. Albert and Waldo stuck themselves in a corner, and so enthralled were they in each other's views that we allowed them space. These two first class brains were at it until 4am. I sneaked off to put up an extra bed.

If you ever hear *Y Tangnefeddwyr* sung by a choir, stop and listen. You also, then, will never forget that great-hearted man of principles, the one and only Waldo.

Goodbye to a Dream

When I finally persuaded my wartime boss, Mr Roy Evans, that World War II had truly finished, I went back to London to follow my dream of becoming a famous writer. I would, of course, come back home at frequent weekends to hang out with the Wayfarers. Things were moving on smoothly. On one weekend, I attended a Wayfarers' dinner at the Black Lion Hotel, New Quay, Cardiganshire. There was always a special welcome there for us from the landlord, Jac Patrick, a flamboyant character and a friend of Dylan Thomas. The guest speaker at the dinner was John Griffiths, the BBC producer at Alexandria Road, Swansea, at the time. I looked forward to a gala night.

I was honoured to be seated next to the guest speaker. We had not met before and I began to suspect that my table companion, an exceedingly tall and handsome fellow, was of a rather nervous disposition. He was assaulting his fingernails ferociously, biting down to the quick. He also kept on repeating that he didn't need any more scripts, that in fact he had enough to last him for at least six months. O.K. So what? I wasn't offering him any. By this time he was making me nervous, too, and I could feel my red hair beginning to tingle. I knew I had to do something so, and as ever, acting first and thinking later, I told him in no uncertain terms: 'Mr Griffiths, if you were the only producer in the whole world, I wouldn't offer you a script'. I gave him what I hope was a courteous nod, and took myself away to the furthest corner of the room for the night. I went home with my thoughts in an incredible twist. The following day there was an enthusiastic appreciation of our guest speaker by all the Wayfarers. He had probably disliked me because I had gone to London to write in English. Did he think, maybe, I was a traitor to my Welshness? I felt a bit uneasy. But then, nobody had ever commissioned me to write anything in Welsh. And I had my dream.

On the Tuesday after the dinner and about to return to London, I received a letter addressed to me with 'BBC Wales' on the outside. It was from Mr John Griffiths asking whether I would submit a script to him. I was being asked in my own country to write a script in my own language. And by a man I had thought impossible! I reminded myself sternly that redheads do not bear grudges. I cancelled London and there and then sat at home and wrote a script. It was accepted. Thereafter for years and years I wrote in Welsh, mainly for BBC Wales, with the occasional story or article for London magazines. I wrote well over a dozen documentaries, mainly about rural life. In those days, it wasn't that easy sticking a microphone under a nose, and then asking questions. No, a documentary in those days meant, more or less, writing a play each time. I tackled all sorts of rural activities – The District Nurse; An Auctioneer; Telephone the Plumber; Call the Vet; Gypsy Life; Harvest Home, etc. There was such a demand for radio programmes before the onslaught of television.

My impossible John Griffiths turned out to be one of the most agreeable and fairest people to work for. After working for the BBC for a while, I understood, from first-hand experience, John's nervousness when we first met. I met one or two women, who were not unknown to me, who would attack like rottweilers in their attempts to have their scripts accepted. He had a heart of gold and would probably have felt uneasy if I had bombarded him with scripts that he would subsequently find unsuitable.

I really enjoyed writing through the medium of Welsh. I was invited to be on the panel of writers that scripted the current radio soap at the time, *Teulu Ty Coch* ('The Red House' – a story of a schoolmaster's family). It ran for some time. When that ended, John Griffiths started a daily soap from Swansea, *Teulu'r Mans* ('The Manse Family'). I was in at its birth and still there when it ended at the height of its glory, six or seven years later.

Teulu'r Mans was absolute fun. It also had a formidable influence on some rural areas. Chapels had to re-arrange services in order that the members would not miss out on an episode. We wrote for years without credits, but, when the listeners were eventually given our names, we were accosted and told whether they agreed or disagreed with how the Manse family lived its life. I can still remember being almost assaulted by two angry ladies on the railway platform at Swansea. The imminent death of the series had been foretold in a local paper. The two ladies came at me, umbrellas poking threateningly and accusing me personally of discontinuing their favourite programme. How could I cut off the story when the minister's wife was about to have a baby and they both had a list of names for the new arrival? I found out, when I managed to have a calm chat with the excited pair, that someone in their village was running a book, and the betting was heavy as to which name would be chosen. Maybe I became their victim because the minister's wife was also called Eluned!

Yes, this is how that happened. We had our first conference, John Griffiths in charge, and the scriptwriters, Jacob Dafis, Ifor Rees and myself in attendance. Jacob and Ifor were both ministers so I was the odd one out. The Manse family were to be the Bowens. We moved on to the wife's name. Before I could make a single suggestion, the two men decided they had an appropriate name – Eluned. After the shock, I applauded their choice. I felt honoured – a minister's wife! I had become a woman of stature. My pride was short-lived. It was decided that this minister's wife did not fit in with my idea of a godly spouse. Eluned Bowen was to be a smoker, a drinker and had all the other vices of that particular time.

To this day, I still find some people who can remember some of the characters we depicted. Among others there was Dilys Davies (a great actress) and her cemented saying *Mersi*

Fach ('Small Mercy!'). This we pinched from the wife of an old character down my way, the rag-and-bone merchant, Moses Vaughan, who would always greet you with '*Mersi* me'.

That most lovable of all performers, Manny Price, became Joe Long. After the series, I think he still went through life as Joe Long. He was built around Sam Morgan (Sam Cwmtawel), who lived outside Cenarth. He used to draw out his conversation so was nicknamed Sam Long, but was a favourite of the villagers. Our Joe Long became an absolute fit. There were so many characters who almost became part of the real community. Mrs Powell y Parce, a snobby bitch, and my closest friend, was played by Lena Williams, whilst Cynddylan Williams, who had always yearned to be a real-life minister, was cast as the Rev. Bowen. Then there was Evie Lloyd, with the gold tooth, a true gentleman of the times. Other writers subsequently joined us, amongst them Eic Davies, Elfyn Talfan, Islwyn Williams and T. Llew Jones among others. I don't know whether the writers, or the listeners, had the more fun. Yes, it was a happy time.

I then went on to television, with soaps like *Y Sgwlyn* and *Y Gwyliwr*, and some one-off plays, one of which I can recall particularly, because it caused me a few sleepless nights. I had been commissioned to script one of the rural short stories of Dr D. J. Williams, Fishguard, that true, charismatic Welshman. One of my favourite actors, Gwenyth Petty, had a leading role. It was a country scene with a live calf that had to be fed. The calf's head got caught in the bucket, which added immensely to the authenticity of the transmission. Gwenyth, a true professional, acted as if she had spent her life feeding calves. But I guess, being the daughter of a colliery official from Maesteg, it was her first time, too, for wearing clogs. It was a splendid performance and I only hope she has forgiven me for landing her in such an unlikely situation.

It is good to remember the good old days!

A Roving Reporter

My London days were over. I pitched into all sorts of things. For a time I became a roving radio reporter, covering South Wales, whilst poet T. Glynne Davies covered North Wales. Going out live could be nerve-racking, but it could also be pure joy. I would get a telephone call from the BBC in Cardiff, suggesting an interview and I would turn the nose of the car towards the venue, hopefully in time to deliver. Variety is the spice of life. Amen to that.

It could be dodgy at times, however. I remember one instance in particular. Cardiff were on the phone, asking me to interview the Charles Brothers in Pencader, near Carmarthen, that night. Who on earth were the Charles Brothers? I rang the BBC back. The girl on the desk answered. She didn't know either and the others were at lunch. I telephoned the Sergeant of Police at Pencader and asked innocently what exciting event was the village hosting that night, hoping to cover up my ignorance. The proud (if rather unhelpful) answer was that the Charles Brothers were there. I had to come clean. The Charles Brothers, I was told, were famous footballers and playing six-a-side that night, so Pencader was over the moon at having attracted such celebrities. Cenarth, unfortunately, was more au fait with poaching (I'll come back to that later) than footballing.

I hurried to Pencader hoping for a miracle. I honestly believe I found it at the Beehive Inn that night. The Charles Brothers, John and Mel, with another soccer celebrity, Ivor Allchurch, were there. It was like the sun's extended smile after the darkness of a black storm. These lovely men enveloped my ignorance, took me out on the field and taught me how to play six-a-side. Through their kindness, the programme, which went

120

out live, must have touched the hearts of many listeners, because the BBC received a call for a repeat. I met John Charles on two or three occasions afterwards and he became my idol for life. He was the most charming gentleman that I was ever fortunate to have known. Sadly, I was out of the country when he died. I would have liked to have said my goodbye, and my sincere thanks for having known him.

This reporting business was exciting. I never knew where I would be from one day to the next. It would be the Weeping Yew at Nevern Church, Pembrokeshire, today, *Dydd Iau Mowr* ('Big Thursday') at Aberporth, Cardiganshire, tomorrow. I could find myself horse racing at Llanon, near Aberystwyth, where that beloved vet, Tommy Herbert, held sway and almost became a programme on his own. Then there was the motor-cycling event at Banc y Warren, Cardigan, where the top racers would always draw crowds and leave me with thundering noises in my head for at least a month afterwards! One top racer there from around Gloucester (his name escapes me at the moment) was a huge draw and he seemed to be jumping miles from one planet to another. I really thought of such bikers when, years later, I was standing before the memorial of the horse in Patagonia, the one that jumped the ravine to freedom. It was exciting and frightening. From shutting my eyes on my first, terrifying visit, I graduated to presenting the trophies. I did not know a single cc cycle from a 100 cc one. I suspect I even held the well-earned trophies upside-down!

There is another event I remember with great joy. There came a call to go and interview Dai Dower, who was boxing at Carmarthen. Again, the innocent abroad, I had never been to a boxing match in my life. I was given a ringside seat. The first class was the heavyweight. I think I disgraced myself when this solid Jamaican came near the ropes and I let forth a piercing yell, thinking he was about to land in my lap! A man sitting next to me, no doubt recognising my imperfect appreciation of the noble art, offered to explain as we went along. He really was a great help, but unfortunately when he got excited, he would grab my knee to get my attention. I have ticklish knees and am inclined to giggle if touched suddenly. I warned the man that the programme was going out live, and that if he kept on causing my giggles, I would name him as my helper. He begged me not to, his wife would not approve and did not know he was at a boxing match. In spite of his best efforts, we did have a giggle or two, resulting in the *Western Mail* receiving a very stern letter of disapproval that the BBC had sent a woman to report at a boxing match, one that seemed to be inappropriately enjoying herself. I guess the giggles did really convey that I was truly having a gleeful time watching two grown men hammering each other. All the same, I think if Mrs Seymour Rees of Seven Sisters, Glamorgan, had been at Dai Dower's particular event, she might have agreed that his dancing powers would not be amiss at a ballet performance. I confess, he was the only boxer I've ever admired, apart from that charismatic Everest of a man, Muhammad Ali.

The broadcasting options became endless. There was BBC, TWW, HTV and, latterly, S4C. I was invited to join panels and to script programmes on Dewi Emrys, Edith Piaf, Augustus John, Picasso, Allen Raine, Gypsies. There were TV portraits: *Llwyd Bach y Baw*; *Luned Bengoch*; *Dan y Wyneb*; *Clymau*; *O Vaughan i Fynwy*; *Mwynhau'r Pethe*; not to mention *On the road with Elinor* after which I was bombarded with telephone calls. Much of that English transmission's appeal had to do with Elinor Jones, an able, charming and professional interviewer who drew in those non-Welsh speakers who wanted to know what the native Welsh speakers were up to. When I watch myself on TV, my main object is to hope for the end and a comforting cup of tea. But that night, the telephone calls were so numerous from 8 o'clock onwards that at quarter to three in the morning I remained still parched. The machine and I needed a rest. I took it off the hook until a restart in the morning.

I think my Gran would have been proud of me. Her 'Have a

go, girl. Give it your best shot' has stood me in good stead a few times when I've been up against it. Like the time I was doing a radio interview for a BBC programme in London at a well-known hostel for down-and-outs. There was an old sea captain from New Quay, Ceredigion, spending some nights there, maybe somewhat intoxicated but still a great character. I found the building, grey, tall, gloomy and forbidding. I looked and looked for a private entrance but could only see a room with a line of rough-looking characters. Well I had to 'have a go', didn't I? So I joined the male unfortunates and moved step by step with them to reach the hatch where an official was handing out chits for a bed for the night. Having a female in their midst was causing more than a bit of commotion. I won't repeat what the startled official said when I popped my head through the hatch. The old lag behind me shouted 'Give her a bed, cock. I'll share it with her.' His homeless companions thought it was hilarious but the official had no sense of humour and I was unceremoniously snatched by two wardens and taken to a private room to interview my fellow *Cardi*. And what a character he was. It was well worth my embarrassment. Beside his rich tales of the old sea dogs who used to hang around the pier at New Quay in the old days, he sang beautifully those two memorable songs sung by the two brothers, Jac a Wil – *Pwy fydd yma 'mhen can mlynedd?* ('Who'll be here in a hundred years?') and *Dwed wrth mam* ('Tell my mother'). I went out to the London fog with the haunting refrains buzzing in my ears and tried to forget my unorthodox entrance in search of a scoop.

Remembering backwards can at times be entertaining and happy. Even some of my embarrassing episodes seem almost normal at this great distance.

Still with itchy feet, after the war I travelled, mainly alone, over tracts of grey land and greyer towns and cities across Eastern Europe. Looking back at those distant years, I admit it was quite unusual for a young woman to do so. Certainly I never found a swarm of back-packers around every corner like

123

today, nor do I remember the modern worries of being attacked. I guess I was taken as the simple country girl I am, with a love of meeting people and with a great curiosity to find out how other people live in remote parts of the world. I travel alone when I can, for having no sense of direction, I am inclined to get lost, which can at times be embarrassing. But mostly tremendous fun. More of that later.

Choirs

One of the best natured and truest friends I ever had was Eira Thomas, married, when I first knew her, to Eirydd Thomas, chemist, then of Llandeilo, in the Tywi valley, Carmarthenshire. A brilliant musician, harpist, pianist, choral conductor and sometime composer, she was a member of the Gorsedd of Bards, music section, first as Telynores Dinefwr, and eventually in her white robes as Eira Dinefwr. I admit that I did not know as much about the musical side of Wales as I should have, as all my spare time was involved with its literary life. Much of that was set to change in 1984 when the Welsh Gorsedd of Bards decided to take a trip over to visit our sister Gorsedd in Llydaw (Brittany).

After meeting on that trip, somehow or other Eira and I spent a lot of time together and found we had a lot of similar interests. She had a great passion for her music, I had a great passion for my literary work. This we found excellent. We both also had this itch for travelling. We became great friends, and remained so until her sudden death in 2002. She was such fun; a person one could never forget. She could at times, too, land me in impish situations. I remember one night, Eira and I were sharing a room in a hotel in Esquel, Patagonia. The windows had shutters and it was a stuffy night. Eira needed more air. We failed to open the shutters so had to call a porter. I told Eira it was her turn to try out her Spanish. She did try but was overtaken by a bout of giggling. I took the phone and managed to convey the service we needed. A smart Spaniard arrived at about 3am. I tried, with the help of my phrase book, to apologise for disturbing him at that unearthly hour but stressed that my friend really had to have air. I turned to Eira in the other bed, to confirm her need. There was nobody in the other bed. Eira, bless her, had hidden herself under the bedclothes. The glint in the Spanish eye told me that he did not believe that there had ever been anyone in the other bed. To Eira's delight, proving otherwise became problematic! Those were hilarious days.

It was Eira who introduced me to the world of choirs. I have always loved music, my piano teacher, Rita Castle House, had made sure of that. Now I was thrown wholeheartedly into all things choral. Eira herself conducted her own choir, the Llandybïe Ladies. They used to compete and I became their mascot. Eira was also the accompanist and répétiteur of the Carmarthen section of Côr Meibion De Cymru (The South Wales Male Voice Choir). I remember her even conducting the whole choir once out in Belgium. The choir visited many countries and Eira and I never missed a trip. It was always fun and a worthwhile experience. The officials and members of the choir gave me such a welcome and, bless them, made me a life member. I remember first meeting the secretary, Ken Crawle and his wife, Joan. What a delight! The loveliest couple I had ever met and, after all these years, they remain so. The president was Lord Gordon Parry of Neyland, Pembrokeshire. I had known of him but had never met him. I knew of him as an orator and idolised his gift from afar. I think it may have been on a trip to Canada with the choir (or maybe it was Belgium, there were so many) that we were being coached from one venue to another. Lord Parry, the president, addressed us. He was relating the story of Prince Madoc of North Wales leading his thirteen little ships reputedly to discover what became America. There is a Welsh poem depicting this epic and Lord Parry couldn't quite remember it. Without thinking, I just reeled it off.

Wele'n cychwyn tair ar ddeg	(Thirteen little ships
o longau bach ar fore teg,	sailed one fine morning
Wele Madoc, dewr ei fron.	with Madoc, stout of heart,

yn gapten ar y llynges hon.	Captain of this fleet.
Mynd yr oedd i roi ei droed	He was on a journey to put his foot
ar le na welodd dyn erioed.	on land not yet seen by man.
Antur enbyd ydoedd hon,	This was a daring adventure,
A Duw a'i deil o don i don.	God will keep him from wave to wave.)

I guess Lord Parry was surprised at this unknown voice, wafting up from the centre of the coach. He came to introduce himself and invited me to share his front seat. We talked and talked. I found him to be one of the most interesting and knowledgeable persons I had ever met. We found common interests in many fields, especially in the workings of the French Resistance during the war. He became a trusted friend. He and Glenys his wife, were a perfect couple. I was waiting on his doorstep, having been invited to lunch, on the morning that we found he had died in the night. There can be no replacement.

Lord Parry could be a teaser at times, too, mind. I remember the choir singing at Cardiff on Sea, near San Diego and we had all been invited by the Marines to dine and be entertained at their depot. It was all new to me. I had never known any marines. Lord Parry was grabbing everyone's attention with an address from the stage, when suddenly he declared 'And now Eluned will take charge of the Marines.' It was a shock like an instant paralysis. The officer in charge invited me to have a seat amongst them. Luckily he had an easy, friendly manner. But the saviour of the night for me, was the Marine mascot. It was a Churchill-lookalike bulldog. After each item of entertainment, before giving any of us a chance, the bulldog would lead the applause. To our great amusement, he did so throughout the night. I argued with my new friends that the dog must have been somehow alerted when to give his impressive howls of applause. In spite of their full co-operation, I failed to discover any way that it could be done. I satisfied myself that even Poirot could not have solved this mystery. I decided that living with the Marines had made the dog human. I have a lot of respect for the Marines ever since.

Another time I was caught out unexpectedly. We were in Australia. Lord Parry was giving an interesting address, as usual. I was listening intently. He was telling his audience about 'little Willie,' a Welshman who had become the Prime Minister of Australia for seven years. It was riveting stuff and I was feeling secretly ashamed that I knew hardly anything about this little man. But our Lord President was in full sail, telling his listeners without any warning that, and I quote, 'Eluned is going to write a television script on little Willie's life.' That was the first I had even heard of this former Prime Minister, whose sayings were turning out to be as spicy as our Lloyd George's sharp tongue. Lord Parry and I discussed it later, and with his ability to delve into the inner soul of a character, not to mention his help and knowledge, I had to admit that it could be an engaging TV portrait. Sadly, we were beaten by time.

I was on cloud nine, being drawn into the bosom of these choirs. I have always thought that music could somehow help to save the world. Not so long ago I said in a broadcast that I thought the Llangollen International Eisteddfod did more for humanity than our great National Eisteddfod. Getting all nations to intermingle and sing together surely would lessen the inevitable fighting for supremacy between different races. Fair play, the chairman of the Llangollen Eisteddfod telephoned me, on hearing the broadcast, offering me free tickets. Some of my fellow National Eisteddfod members, however, thought I had committed treason and I gathered their choice would have been to lead me before a firing squad. Ah, well. Maybe I'm naive. But I remember, years ago, listening to Martin Luther King's 'I have a dream' speech. And his voice, and his plea for humanity, even now, still clings to my ear drums as if I was wearing one of those multi-advertised, digital earpieces.

The South Wales Male Voice Choir became my favourite glee singers. I came to know them all as friends. There was no member from my immediate area but I did know two very

Initiation into *Gorsedd y Beirdd* ('the Bardic Circle') at the Fishguard National Eisteddfod, 1936. I am second from left in the front row.

A studio portrait, 1950s.

Another studio portrait, 1960s.

Being crowned at the Gŵyl Fawr Cardigan eisteddfod in 1966.

Admiring my first National crown in the company of Dilys Cadwaladr,
the first woman ever to win a National crown.

Being escorted by Erfyl Fechan to the stage to be crowned
at the National Eisteddfod in Bala in 1967.

The crowning ceremony at Bala.

A royal welcome back to Cenarth after the 1967 National Eisteddfod. It was organised by Wyn Jenkins, Penwern Farm, and Mr Williams, Gorslas.

More 1967 village celebrations led by the vicar, Rev. Stephens.

Celebrating my second National Crown, Llangefni 1983.

Two crowns, one head.

With Pierre Loisel, the Breton Bardic
Circle's *Bardd Mawr*, Archdruid.

With a portrait of George Bernard
Shaw in Dublin.

With an original boomerang
in Australia.

With Linda Kinsey in on my
favourite island, Sentosa.

Linda Kinsey's first portrait of me.
A very solemn pose!

With Eira and two airline pilots, celebrating my 80th birthday in Santa Monica.

With my Good Samaritan
border guard in Chile.

With Police Superintendent
Glen Harrison escorting me to
Chinatown in Sydney.

Leading a pedigree Patagonian bull with our driver, Maldwyn.

On the bull's back in Buenos Aires, aided and abetted by D. Ben Rees,
Liverpool, with his hand over the bull's eye!

energetic songsters – two friends, Jac Davies (of Jac and Wil fame) of Cefneithin, Cross Hands, and Alun James of Llanarthne. We happened to be out in California at the same time, once: Alun and his wife, Eira, Jac, Eira Thomas and myself. Wonderful company. In fact I am eternally grateful to Jac. His long legs saved me from drowning in a private pool belonging to some friends in Palos Verdes. I don't know whether he regretted his Samaritan act afterwards. If he did, he has always been too much of a gentleman to broadcast it. Perhaps that gives weight to my infallible belief that music can conquer most of the trivialities of this galloping-to-disaster world of ours.

When I first settled amongst them, their conductor was the charismatic Dr Haydn James, originally from Nantyffyllon, Maesteg, but London-based for years. I love laughter and Haydn and I have managed to laugh on all our distant travels. His sense of humour is a must-be-protected gift. He is a doctor of physics, too, so at times we have to be in awe. With a string of conducting commitments in and around London, Haydn's expertise in conducting massed choirs and vast audiences is internationally established. He has led the singing of up to 75,000 spectators at Wembley and at Cardiff's Millennium Stadium, and conducted the British Lions Male Choir in Australia in 2001. (And I would like to add 'I was there'). That same choir was reformed to tour New Zealand with the British and Irish Lions in June/July 2005, ending with a concert at Sydney Opera House.

What is more, Dr Haydn is regularly invited to conduct *cymanfaoedd canu* (hymn-singing festivals) at home and abroad, and has made a significant contribution to choral singing in the London Welsh community, notably as musical director of the London Welsh Male Voice Choir.

And here I am bursting to tell you a snippet that will probably label me truly egotistic. In 2007, Haydn James was, as usual, conducting the annual Thousand Voices Concert at the

Royal Albert Hall, and included in his repertoire Michael J. Lewis's magnificent composition 'Cenarth', a setting of one of my hymns. It was a thrill to hear it that evening, especially with the introduction that was played by the Welsh Guards' Band.

I had been invited as a guest to the reception and concert, and was accompanied by my long-time friend and evergreen eisteddfod companion, Trixie Smith, a one-time great soprano from Llandovery. She, Ruth Price and, sadly, the late Eirwen, a doctor's wife, were always there for me when I was chosen to greet the winning bard at a National Eisteddfod, the pillars that vetted my hastily written verses in case I would lash out too sarcastically at the men who never gave a woman the chance of becoming an Archdruid. All in good fun of course. Ruth Price was a top BBC producer who could recite '*Pwllderi*' even better than the author himself, Dewi Emrys. Amazing. But I'm straying again. So what of that reception?

What a wonderful time Trixie and I were having, meeting new and old friends, notably that riotous pantomime dame, Wyn Calvin and his wife Carol, who kept an eye on my comfort all night. I was so thrilled that the president, Cliff Morgan, whom I have admired for years, especially his outstanding orations, had made such an effort to be with us in spite of his illness. We certainly missed out on his unique ability to address us, but the warmth of his kiss will instead remain with me for years to come. May God bless and take care of a man so well liked by everyone.

If I'm out of my depth, I am always thankful to follow like a lamb. So Trixie and I climbed the stairs. It was turning out to be a very special night. In total surprise and awe, we were led to the Royal Box. I was offered the Queen's seat and sat in thrill and confusion. I was trying to work things out: Trixie next to me must be sitting in Prince Philip's usual place. It took me a while to compose myself even to be slightly royal. Trixie, having a more commanding personality, took our elevation in her stride. Sharing our box was the very sociable Deputy Mayor of London and his lovely wife. Not since I did my first bit on stage in our Cenarth village hall (when I bared all) had I felt so bemused and important. Looking round the great sold-out hall and fixing my eyes on the pageant of colour weaved by the choristers with their varied coloured jackets, I found it as compelling as seeing the Bayeux Tapestry for the first time.

The smooth running of the evening was in the hands of that capable and gracious master of ceremonies, Frank Lincoln. Even when he split on me and told the audience that when he had asked if he could divulge that I was 93 years old, I had given him a sharp 'No' since I was only 92 the following Friday, I still think he is a fine performer and when he disclosed that I was sitting in the Queen's seat, my niece sitting in the audience told me she swelled with pride.

And our Dr Haydn James did make it an extra, extra special night for me. I had never heard 'Cenarth' sound so inspiring. It was a concert par excellence and I hope that *Calonnau ar Dân* ('Hearts afire') extended its message to all who heard it and that all the resounding choruses stayed with us for a very long time. A night never to be forgotten.

There really is something about choirs and conductors that can uplift us. The present conductor of Côr Meibion De Cymru is another gem. A Llanelli boy, Eifion Thomas is a champion tenor as well as a fine conductor. I had known him from afar as the conductor of the Llanelli Male Voice Choir, forever taking top prizes at the National Eisteddfod. He never stops amazing me. Found him once on TV standing up to that doubly-sharpened battleaxe, Anne Robinson, in her *The Weakest Link* programme – and winning. Then out with the choir in Eastern Europe last year, I discovered he was no mean poet. I was honoured when he showed me a poem he had just written on our visit to Auschwitz. It touched every nerve in that mindless desolation:

131

Ni chân yr adar mwy
yn nistawrwydd y gwacter
llethol
sydd o gwmpas yr anialwch
bydol hwn,
a grewyd gan orchymyn
rhyw deyrn gwallgofus

(The birds no longer sing
in the silence of the
emptiness
around this worldly
wilderness
created at the command of
an insane dictator.

Ond cryfach yw'r cariad
Sy'n enaid y fam a'r tad
Na'r arswyd
Sy'n enaid y plentyn . . .
cryfach yw
na' r nwy a'r dryll.
Hwn bydd fyw'n
Dragwyddol.'

But the love is stronger
in the soul of the mother and father
Than the terror
in the soul of the child . . .
It is stronger than
the gas and the gun.
It will live
eternally.)

Another person who helped me at that wall of death with a short, impressive address that eased my confused and bruised mind was our present choir president, Wyn Calvin M.B.E. I can see his stance now, his clear, quiet voice and hand outstretched as if saving us all from the horror of horrors. It brought back to me a time when I was in Israel. I had gone by myself to the museum where they were depicting the massacre of the innocent children. The place was in utter darkness. It became so real that the small electric light bulbs became the eyes of the children peering at me. The music became the groans of the victims. I became so engrossed in the tragedy that my legs became paralysed. I groped at the railing to try to get to the exit the other end. I was finding it, step by step, very difficult. Someone behind me, caught my shoulder to help and we managed to move in the darkness to the opening and daylight. I turned to thank the person who had helped me. He was a young man. I realised that through his tears he was speaking German. I understood 'I am ashamed. I am ashamed.' Somehow I felt a glimmer of hope.

Yes, there are bonuses in being accepted a friend of the South Wales Choir. As well as the names of Wyn Calvin and his lovely, interesting wife, Carol, I would like to add another member of the choir who managed to boost my slithering confidence: the impressive Paul Robeson-voiced John Adams of Cwmbrân. He came down to Cenarth to record a reading of a selection of my poems, twenty-eight of them, I think. It was decided to do the recording in my chapel, Bryn Seion, and on a day when a new Ice Age seemed imminent. Anyone listening to the recordings must have thought we were in the Dan-yr-Ogof caves. Indeed, you could feel the stalactites hanging from my tongue. But John Adams knew his craft. Surprisingly those select persons who have listened to the effort have responded with enthusiasm, clamouring for more. I may just agree to that if time permits. It really was a boost. I have never been good at discussing poetry publicly, having always thought that prayer and poems are personal and private. But the response was remarkable. One doctor wrote to tell me that hearing my bilingual attempts had made him seriously set out to learn the Welsh language. Such responses, along with my commitment to working bilingually in America, have given me such joy.

Sadly, John died shortly after the recordings were made, but I was privileged to be invited to say my goodbye at his funeral, and continue to hope that my closing sentiments on that day remain some comfort to his beloved Ruth and his numerous friends:

> Seiniau a ddeil i'n swyno –
> Ei lais coeth o Lys y Co'.

> ('Sounds that remain to charm us –
> his rich voice from the Mansion of Memories.')

Before finishing with my attachment to the choir, I must add one special person to my roll call. Dr Mair Williams, so deservedly appointed High Sheriff of Glamorgan, is an absolute treasure and, as the choir's medical overseer on their travels, has made life comfortable for so many of the members. I find her so inspiring. She has never made me feel my age. I remember about two years ago I was invited to be the choir's guest at a dinner at Folly Farm, near Tenby. I had my niece with me. We were passing through the amusement part of the farm when Dr Mair spotted us. She caught my hand and away we went for a ride on the merry-go-rounds. I was almost ninety years of age, flying sky high. Way down below I could see Annie, my niece, her face convulsed with terror. She couldn't have looked more agonised had she been face to face with a growling tiger. My only worry, however, was my slip-on shoes falling off as I had not bargained for such high jinks. When we returned to terra firma, Annie, eyes still bulging with amazement, did not reproach her very old aunt, nor the doctor who so enjoyed flying through the air with her! It was a lesson my really very nice niece took to heart when she came with me last year touring Budapest, Prague and Krakow, following me meekly along and up the seeming thousands of miles and steps that we walked and climbed. All the same, remembering Picasso and our debate about his depiction of his portrayal of the ugly woman, it would be too daring to look in mirrors as I pass by.

Australia and the Irish

They say that travelling is a bug. If so, I must have contracted it quite badly! My early expeditions may well have been unusually intrepid for a girl brought up in rural Cardiganshire, especially since they were undertaken alone. In later life, however, the adventures have had the safety of numbers to recommend them, but have been no less exciting.

It was thanks again to Côr Meibion De Cymru that I had my first taste of Australia. I had my friends Linda and Stan staying with me at the time. You haven't met them yet, so hang on: Linda was Tonypandy, Stan was Treorchy; they met and got married. What a great mix! They don't have to explain their origins anywhere in the world. Two words suffice: Rhondda valley.

I first met Linda years back. She's a first-class artist, now living in Ontario, Canada and Cymer, Rhondda. She was going around Wales doing a series of portraits of poets and Welsh craftsmen. She had just completed an excellent portrait of Denzil the coracleman, who lives in Cenarth and attends the same chapel as I do. Denzil told her she ought to come and see me if she was doing poets. She telephoned. We arranged a meeting. She painted a portrait. A very good one, but one of a very serious-looking me, on my best behaviour, looking sedate and uncommunicative! After all I had never been invited to sit for a professional painter before. The seriousness didn't last long, however. We got to know each other and we've been cheerful friends since. She executed a really good portrait of me a few years ago, one of me in my bardic gown, and one that has subsequently been hanging around Cardiff venues for some time. She did a special one of the choir's late president, Lord

135

Gordon Parry. She is at the moment also finishing one of our present president, Wyn Calvin, and one of our Doctor Mair, the High Sheriff. She's amazing and can capture an almost photographic likeness in about half an hour. And she started off as a qualified electronic engineer. Beat that!

Linda was staying with me when I said I was going to Australia with the choir. Linda said she would like to go and Stan jumped in and said he had one of his school friends living out there. So we all decided to go. Linda and Stan are a great pair to have around socially and made a special trip even more enjoyable. Just being in the Sydney Opera House listening to the choir under their conductor, Dr Haydn James, would have been tremendous value, but there were endless other attractions. I even made a true aborigine friend, one Goom Blar, who comes occasionally to Cardiff for the rugby matches. I felt special. He allowed me to play his didgeridoo. Not that my musical attempt had an impressive impact. Before I left, he found our coach and presented me, much to the envy of my fellow travellers, with his own native boomerang, autographed. I think people have been extra careful with me since, in case I use that boomerang to get rid of my enemies.

Anyway, we did all the things we wanted to, and a few things I didn't particularly want to. Stan and Lin have a passion for sightseeing in cable cars. I have a passion for keeping as far way as possible from these contraptions. Admittedly, there was one cable-car ride that I count amongst my favourite excursions ever, the one that took me to a little island of (man-made) paradise outside Singapore. It had an intriguing cave of spices and peacocks, unblushingly displaying their extended colourful tails. It was so, so peaceful, my Sentosa dream island. I remember when I was about ten and very romantic, writing a lyric, called 'My Dream Isle', which somebody sent away to be set to music. And, here, all those years later, I had found it. If I had money and time, I would settle for spending six months of every year in this Eldorado. But my view of cable cars changed when I was caught in one once in Switzerland, and dangled in thin air for two hours. So when I now enter a cable car, I sit stiffly with my eyes tightly shut.

It's amazing how one incident can dent your confidence forever. I am terrified of water, too. I was three or four years old and had a dislocated shoulder falling off my pony, Edward I. We went to our local seaside resort, Aberporth, with my play mates, Willie Cilfod and Emlyn Cilfod Fach. These two big older boys threw me into the waves. Even if I had known how to swim, I only had one healthy arm – and that was flailing around like a cow's tail whipping bloodthirsty flies. Ever since, I have kept my distance from water, too.

Linda and Stan went to stay with Stan's school friend for a few days, so when the eagle eyes looking after me so efficiently were far away, as usual, my freedom led me astray. Sydney is full of warm-hearted people, who are friendly and fun. But beware of an Irish speaker who has kissed the Blarney Stone many, many times. He reminded me of that never-to-be-forgotten great folk-song collector, Seamus Ennis, whose radio programme 'As I Roved Out' was a highlight of our listening for years. I'm sorry I'm side-tracking again but I know you would have liked him, too.

Seamus Ennis and I went around Wales collecting old Welsh folk songs in the 1950s. He was working then in BBC London. He came to stay at my home for three days and was still with us five weeks later. He was one of the most charismatic men I ever met. In chasing old folk songs before they completely disappeared, I think he took me to every pub in west Wales. He had the most uncanny way of persuading quite old characters to sing old folk songs that few of us present had ever heard before. As in the case of the true piper of Hamelin, there would be a string of human beings following him into these country pubs the moment they heard the call of his pipes. He was a well-known uilleann piper, broadcaster, and folklore and music collector, born in May 1919 in Finglas, a rural area of North County Dublin.

Seamus's stories were always funny, heart-warming and numerous. He learnt to play the pipes from his father, James Ellis, a civil servant and a prize-winning musician on several instruments, notably at the Oireachtas (an equivalent festival to our Welsh eisteddfod). His set of pipes had an interesting history. In 1908 his father found them in a sack, in pieces, in a pawnbroker's shop in London and bought them for a small sum of money. After loving care and repair, they turned out to be a set made by the famous Coyne of Dublin in the early years of the 19th century. Their tone when played by Seamus was distinctive and beautiful.

This lover of all things Irish was employed for years at the Three Candle Press, Dublin, performing all the usual tasks associated with the printing trade, as well as learning to write down slow airs and dance music in staff notation. When, in 1942, the Second World War caused shortages in printing materials, he was hired by Professor Seamus O' Duilearge of the Irish Folklore Commission as a folk-music collector and sent to Connemara with pen, paper and pushbike on a salary of £3.00 a week. He wrote down his first song from a man working on the roadside between Oranmore and Galway city. He then got a job with Radio Eireann, leaving at the beginning of the 1950s to work in London with Brian George, a BBC producer who was setting up a scheme to record extensively the surviving folk culture of England, Scotland, Wales and Ireland. Seamus was not a city lover and went back to his grass roots when he finished with BBC London in 1958. He continued to travel around Ireland playing music, and presenting programmes on the new TV station, Teilifis Eireann. He also played at the Newport Folk Festival, U.S.A. He came home to settle finally in a mobile home which he called 'Easter Snow', on land which once belonged to his grandfather, and died in 1982.

How he loved to drive on the roads of Ireland in an old Ford Zephyr, but being his passenger was a rather hairy experience as he would wave to endless friends while relating fascinating stories of places, tunes, songs, players and singers. His willingness to impart his great store of knowledge and piping skills was extraordinary. His collection of music and songs is a major legacy to this day. He was an excellent communicator and enveloped everyone, especially children, in his Irish charisma.

So, after a typically Ennis-like detour, back to my tale of Australia! My Sydney Irishman had the same effect and with my red hair always tangoing at the wrong times, I simply blotted out the scary heights and walked the Sydney bridge with him.

Ireland and its characters has always fascinated me. If I had to live in a country other than Wales, it would be Ireland. They seem to be able to hang on to their characters better than Wales. My landlady in the Bayswater attic, where I aspired to be a writer, was Irish with a heart of gold. And I was so lucky in the 1950s to have met Brendan Behan – and his brother Dominic, too. I even saw two of Brendan's plays, *The Quare Fellow* and *The Hostage*, both produced by Joan Littlewood. He was my rebel of rebels at the time. I think it was Kenneth Tynan who said that he 'kicked English drama from the past into the present.' He was a great wit and raconteur, never at a loss for words. Asked by a TV interviewer 'Do you hate policemen?', his considered answer was 'I don't hate anybody, but I have never seen a situation so dismal that a policeman couldn't make it worse.'

Brendan was a product of his environment. Even before he was ten years old he had joined the Fianna, the IRA youth group and began writing rebel publications. When he was sixteen, he landed himself in prison for 'his determination as an Irish person to regain every inch of our national territory.' If you have read his book *The Borstal Boy* you will have recognised how his nationalistic cause got him into a reform prison. You will also have recognised his talent as a writer. Sentenced again to prison for fourteen years after a shoot-out to prevent detectives arresting an IRA man in Dublin, he found a friend there who encouraged his writing. The Irish language became an obsession and he became so fluent that he wrote his plays *The Hostage* and *A Fine Day in the Graveyard* in Gaelic, as he did all his poetry.

Brendan was released from prison in a Christmas amnesty in 1943 and his literary life began to become noticed. He went to Paris for a year and came under the influence of writers of the calibre of Jean Paul Sartre, Jean Genet, Samuel Beckett and others. When his plays were staged in London, Brendan Behan became a much toasted celebrity. I felt privileged to have met him at that time. He became an instant success in Ireland, England and America. *The Quare Fellow* opened in New York and Brendan became the lovable Irish character entertaining millions on American television. He died much too young at 41 years of age in a Dublin Hospital. Typically, his last words to the nuns standing over his bed were 'God bless you, may your sons all be bishops.'

The Irish are so friendly. This was never better demonstrated than when my friend Eira and I were over in Dublin. It was for a football match, I think. There was a crowd in the hotel, as some well-known Irish singers were being promoted. A young man came over and asked whether he could sit in the chair beside me. I agreed but couldn't understand why, as there were plenty of empty chairs where most of the young people were gathered. He was a pleasant young man and we chatted away. In the end my curiosity got the better of me and I asked why he had chosen to waste his time talking to possibly the oldest person in the room. His reply was pure blarney: 'I don't like being bored. I looked round the room and found you must be the most interesting person here.' I gave him a shirty look. He added ' Who else would wear a Picasso coat at your age?' I forgave him. It was a chilly night and I had grabbed a Picasso coat given to me in America, and thrown it round my shoulders. I ended up, with Eira's help, promoting three brand new records. He and I became lifelong friends, and he sends me artistic cards on all holidays.

I'm sorry if I've muddled up my readers again. The Irish have that effect. I was trying to discuss Australia, so, please, no hard feelings.

After Sydney Harbour Bridge, I looked for more freedom and fun. I found my Llandovery girls: Trixie, Blodwen, Ann, Margaret, along with Rhydwen and Betty and Eric of Cwmann, who seems always to be around like a guardian angel. I think we probably painted Sydney harbour red over the next couple of days. My minister is a Llandovery boy so I knew they wouldn't lead me to a sinful recount. One night we decided we wanted to go to the Chinatown area of the city. But no one knew where it was. So, very conveniently, I asked a Superintendent of Police – if in doubt, go straight to the top! He was a charmer, offered me his arm in a rather Victorian way, walked us a very long way to the best Chinese restaurant in the whole of Australia. Thinking of that uniformed Samaritan has reminded me of another uniformed person who helped me out once in far away Chile. To South America then!

Patagonia

We were in Patagonia in 1997. Eira and I were there, not with a choir this time, but in a group led by the Rev. Ben Rees, Liverpool, and T. Gwynn Jones, North Wales, that distingished and stalwart musician. On that long journey, Eira and I somehow got separated. I was sitting between two charming, but unfamiliar, ladies, which was OK because I like meeting people. The one on my right-hand side was anxious for me to help her complete a limerick, of all things. I'm not very good at this type of verse but we had a lot of fun. The lady on my left was fidgeting. I thought she had lost something so offered to help. She was concerned because she had forgotten to bring her medication for thyroid with her. When I saw she was really disturbed, I tried to ease her worry by telling her that we had a doctor looking after the group and she would get a prescription to cover what she had forgotten to bring. I even offered to go to find the Doctor. 'I know, ' she said, 'I am the Doctor.' Oops! All went well in the end, and we spent some wonderful weeks out there. Most people we met were of Welsh extraction, and the warmth of their welcome put our much-vaunted homeland welcome to shame. And all this in a country where inflation stood at over one thousand per cent.

We trooped to the famous steak bar in Buenos Aires and were served steaks fatter than double encyclopaedias. The Rev. Ben was sitting next to me. I gave one look at my plate and asked Ben if he could eat three quarters of my steak, too. I hate waste. An obliging fellow, he agreed immediately and thoroughly enjoyed it – along with the two helpings of his own. He has had three heart by-passes, but remains a great and lovely companion.

I have been in two minds whether to tell you about something steak-related that happened to me a few years ago. I wasn't going to bore you. But I think it is only fair to issue a meaty warning. I was checking in at Heathrow for my flight to Los Angeles. There was a lot of whispering behind the scenes. Officials stared at me and spoke surreptitiously into their phones. I began to feel like a suspected criminal. I thought they were going to refuse to let me board. I went systematically through my invisible sins. Couldn't or wouldn't confess to any. Eventually, when I was almost on the verge of my first ever bout of depression, I was greeted by a dream-sunrise smile as someone said I was being taken up to the Virgin VIP lounge. I didn't know there was a gossip grapevine at airports, but somehow the desk had been alerted that I was passing through to celebrate my ninetieth birthday in California. I was offered, but politely refused, champagne (I simply don't like it). I accepted a meal, and chose a simple one. There was such a welcome all around. The attendant placed an enticing meal before me. But there were so many genuine smiles on faces that I didn't have the heart to point out that it wasn't what I had asked for. I ate it. It was delicious. I felt like one of the top footballers' wives – nothing was too good for me. Didn't have to worry about a thing. The tannoy would alert me of the time to board.

I walked to the plane almost as regally as the Queen on her eightieth birthday. The moment I entered the plane, I felt a terrific pain somewhere in my foot. I took to silent thinking. No, I hadn't stubbed it, nor had there been anyone around to tread on it. I found my seat – posher than usual. I'd been upgraded, bless them. I reassured myself that I had not had any champagne, no wine, indeed no alcohol at all. The pain was insistent and irritating. I never have trouble travelling. I shook my head and decided to go to the stewardesses for a glass of water. Maybe this surprising fuss was going to my head. When I got there, someone noticed that I was wriggling as I tried to put my foot on the floor. In a second I was surrounded: everybody

143

was trying to help. The flight manager came – but I could only tell them it was a mysterious pain. The manager offered me his arm. I thought he was taking me back to my seat, but no, I arrived in a compartment with two reclining seats. The plane eventually took off and there were twelve hours to go. I don't think Prince Charles could have wished for more favours. I was fed with cheesecakes and other unheard-of goodies. I hate to confess to the number of teas I swallowed. Still the pain was really biting. And after being in two serious car crashes, I have learnt to be stoic about pain. There was no doctor on board. They contacted one outside but my pain remained a mystery. They found me a companion to sit in the other chair – a very interesting pharmacist, a native of South Africa who worked in Los Angeles. The flight manager almost lived with me, the pilot came to visit me five times. On the fifth visit, I asked him who was looking after the plane. Pain or not, we had a good laugh. I was told that the paramedics would be waiting for me on landing and I would be taken to a doctor. I told them I was staying with friends, and even if I wanted to object to a doctor, they would carry me to one regardless.

There were six strong and hearty paramedics waiting at the LAX airport. The spokesman asked me what medication I was on. I answered 75g Aspirin. He again asked me. Three times he asked and I gave the same answer. In the end, the roots of my once-red hair almost burst into flames. I told him in clipped pronunciation that in my country it is 75 grammes of Aspirin. In your country here it is I believe 81 grammes He still shook his head and muttered something about meaning medication. I gave up. I was worried that my friends waiting for me would be alarmed at seeing everyone except me getting through. I wanted to tell my friends, Dafydd and Olive, who had been there for me since my very first venture to America, seventeen years ago, that I was O.K. The pilot and the flight manager got to them before me. Somebody else collected my luggage from the carousel.

144

I have never had such VIP treatment. But I was really baffled. We went to the doctor first thing in the morning. A lovely lady. Her first question was, strangely, 'Have you been eating steak'? I really thought she was the mad one. I told her that I hadn't eaten steak since I'd been in Patagonia years before. Then I remembered that delicious plate of lunch that I'd eaten but had belonged to somebody else. I admitted rather shamefacedly that I'd stolen someone's lunch and there might have been a little steak in that. But what had that to do with a pain in my foot? She smiled and answered. 'In your toe. You have gout.' I almost needed an ambulance there and then, such was my shock.

I had never known anybody with gout. I thought it only happened to royal feasters like Henry VIII. Since then I have learned that it does happen to lesser mortals. The doctor gave me some tablets. By noon I was back to normal. Retribution for snatching somebody's lunch? Yes, and justified, I think. My conscience is still uneasy thinking of the simple meal the man I had cheated had to put up with instead of the rich meal I had gobbled illegally. A tormenting punishment, gout is possibly the worst pain one can have, according to a pain-specialist friend of the family I was staying with. The surprising thing is that it disappeared so quickly, and has never reappeared in the four years since. So that should be a warning not to eat steak when flying. On the other hand it could secretly become a way of getting VIP treatment. But still, there should be a permanent law against pinching another man's lunch.

Meanwhile, back to Patagonia, where it was difficult to avoid superior barbecue steaks and Spanish-Welsh hospitality. It is an amazing country. They will keep smiling and entertaining even when most of them have to hold down three jobs a day to survive. A country full of surprises too, like the leather factory in Buenos Aires. I love leather, and marched in knowing that, passing through, I would not have a hope of being fitted with a leather outfit. I talked to a very pleasant supervisor. A beckoning finger brought the measuring brigade. I was measured for a jacket and skirt in the kind of softest leather normally only pictured in dreams. I was invited to a lounge, served with delicious coffee and given a stack of magazines, enlightening me about the country I was visiting. Soon, very soon in fact, my suit was ready for a fitting to see that I was entirely satisfied with the work. I must have looked a complete zombie as I thought of the weeks of waiting I would have had to endure, if I had ordered a tailored outfit even in an ordinary material back home! I still have that wonderful leather suit that was completed in a coffee break.

But what of Chile?

Over the years, I have celebrated my birthdays in so many unexpected places. I have had choirs singing to me at Niagara Falls, socialised in Cwm Afon and, even once in a while, been at home in Cenarth! I have drunk green tea in Marrakesh and had a snake dancing to me to the tune of its charmer, Abdel Mahmoud. Once I was surrounded by Flamenco gypsy dancers in a cave at the edge of the Perdu mountain in the wilds of Spain, and I remember also being taken to the Opera at La Scala, Milan, to hear *Le Nozze di Figaro*. Then there was the famous ninetieth birthday bash in California, the grand finale by any standard. There were others, too, but I really must stop looking backwards in this muddled script, or Lot's wife's fate awaits me. Such meanderings are the stock-in-trade of the topsy-turvy.

So back to Chile. We were a little group in Esquel, Patagonia. Ann Owen (a member of the Gorsedd) and her husband, Maldwyn, Myra Tycroes, from near Ammanford, and my friend Eira and myself. Somehow they seemed to be ganging up on me that night, trying to keep me prisoner in my room. So be it. If that was their wish, I was quite happy with my own company. Still it was odd, I thought. Next morning, I understood what had been afoot. It was October 27, my birthday, and they had, the previous night, been arranging a birthday surprise for me. And what a surprise! They had hired a car to take me up the Andes. I forgave and forgot immediately.

Ann's husband was in charge of the car and the four women. We were waved off in style by the other members of the party. The snow-capped Andes were a picture. We drove up miles and miles, having the road tracks almost to ourselves. The call of nature became a bit of a problem. But not that much of a problem really, as we hadn't seen any traffic for hours. So we decided on our spot. But, as always in life, the unexpected happened. Three lorries and two cars appeared as on a film track. We did bring photographs back home but they are not displayed openly in any of our lounges. Our waving back to the passing drivers was, to say the least, a little sheepish.

We pushed on. Our driver deserved a knighthood. He drove the car on to the raft to cross the Rio Grande. The waves almost rolled over us, but the birthday spirits affected all. When we reached the Chile checkpoint, our hired car was in real need of hospital treatment. Every part of its anatomy was in distress. The exhaust pipe was dragging along the rough track, making ominous noises. And we were up against two Chilean checkpoint guards. They had no English, we had no Spanish. They sent for their boss. He was charming and looked superior in his smart uniform. I tried to make him understand that we would like the exhaust pipe tied up and even caught hold of his belt to give him a clue. In the end he gave me a broad smile and took the exhaust pipe off. It is still there. I had hoped to go back some time but the years seem to pass at double speed when you get to my age. If anybody ever reads this and goes to the Andes (and I'd recommend every single person who can to make the trip), perhaps you could recover our exhaust pipe. All the way back to Esquel, we had all and sundry waving, smiling and pointing to where the pipe used to be. In fact, how they took the hired car back without being compensated, baffles me. It was a skeleton. It had no handbrake, no spare tyre, no exhaust pipe, but thanks to our special driver, Maldwyn, we arrived back in excellent spirits.

But did we get to Chile, after all? Well, I, for one, wasn't going to turn around willingly without getting my feet on

Chilean soil. But, as the smiling officer pointed out: I didn't even have a passport. Because I had been kidnapped on this treat to the Andes, it was back in the hotel in Esquel! Sometimes, however, the powers above are kind to idiots. We somehow managed to sell the idea that I was having my birthday. The officer's eyes X-rayed me. I guess he came to the conclusion that I was too stupid to be a terrorist, so let me in. Believe me, he became a hero. I was honoured to have my photograph taken with him. That is one photograph that can always be on display in my Glyn-y-Mêl.

Believe it or not, we had one more extra treat on the way back. We knew that there was a cafe in Trefelin called *Nain Maggie*, opened by people from North Wales, who came out on the *Mimosa* (*Nain* is the North Wales word for grandmother). We made our way there and found it. The present owners were very apologetic. Though they were related to the first settlers, sadly they did not speak the Welsh language. My friends told them of my birthday treat. Soon we were sitting round a table, loaded with all sorts of delicacies. They produced a birthday cake with one candle held by a ballet dancer. I still treasure it at home. The owner asked to be excused. We ate as much as we could but realised that we couldn't possibly do justice to such a loaded treat. The gentleman came back with a rather elderly lady. He presented her with a flourish:' This is Mrs. Williams. She speaks Welsh.' He had gone down two streets to bring her to meet us. We invited her to join our birthday party. She tucked in heartily, which to us was a bonus, for with their great generosity, they were always pleased to see a cleared table. Our trip to Patagonia may have been a little sad at times because of their difficulties, but without doubt it was a truly inspiring one.

I even met Carlos Menem, the then President. We came back to our Chubut hotel one night to find two armed guards outside the front door entrance. The place seemed to have been taken over by the military. You can imagine what that did to my ever-ready-to-flame red hair. Did the Argentina Government think that the Welsh, who had taken over the hotel for our stay, had to be subdued by the military? I pitched into the man standing next to me. He listened courteously and then explained. The military were there temporarily because President Menem had a prearranged meeting at our hotel. I became interested. It turned out that the man I had picked for my misguided attack was the President's lawyer. We ended up discussing the eisteddfod being held the following day. I told him all about our eisteddfod back home. He had a forgiving nature and introduced me to the President. Both he and the President turned up at the eisteddfod next day, and both men actually approached for another little chat. I was honoured, too, to be called to greet the winning bard at their own very successful annual eisteddfod. After all, competing at eisteddfodau was something I knew quite a bit about . . .

The Competitive Years

I don't remember a time when I wasn't competing at local eisteddfodau. I was forever scribbling at the eleventh hour, and keeping my mother out of bed, too, because if she wasn't guarding me at the end, she probably thought I would be up all night. Too true. It's an annoying habit I never grew out of unfortunately.

I used to compete in all classes in the literary section. I used to recite, too. We used to receive some wonderfully-designed prize bags to carry our meagre money prizes. With two or three of those round my neck after a night's competing, I felt even more excited, I guess, than I would if I won the lottery today. The first prize I remember winning was for a drawing of a donkey.

When I got a bit older, I would compete in the Urdd eisteddfodau, evidence of which I discovered in the attic when we were preparing to move to the bungalow: a whole stack of certificates and book prizes. At one eisteddfod, I apparently won five prizes in the poetry section. When I was at Cardigan Grammar School, I was always inspired to compete by our very able Welsh mistress, Miss Mona Hughes. She was also the one who urged me to recite at the Caerphilly National Urdd Eisteddfod. The set-piece was in the old Welsh strict metre, and Mrs Clement Davies, who taught me *cynghanedd*, had given her blessing. A few children from the school went to the eisteddfod and we were billeted with various families. I was staying in a council house. In the night, the ceiling collapsed. I was unhurt, but the confusion and the dust brought on a persistent cough. So Caerphilly and the nation never got to hear me! Soon I was packed off to London and that ended my competing for years. Later when I came back to Wales and started writing in Welsh, there were too many exciting projects to find time for eisteddfodic work.

Oddly enough, in the 1960s, I was spending more time at home than usual. Aunty Hannah was nearing her tenth decade and needed extra care after fracturing her femur in a fall trying to avoid hurting a cat. I began writing some poems to keep me active and awake. Browsing one night through the 1963 National Eisteddfod programme, I saw that the subject for the Crown poem was *Y Bont* ('The Bridge'). I immediately saw my bridge. My mother was a collector of Willow Pattern ware. The Welsh dresser in the cottage down the garden was top heavy with it. I didn't know the exact story but I had always been romantically interested in it. I wrote a poem in vers libre, a form I was happily dabbling in at the time having been inspired by reading T. Glynne Davies's *Adfeilion* and W.J. Gruffydd's *Ffenestri*. So for the first time ever I sent in an entry to the National Eisteddfod. I told my big sister Get, but no one else. I knew I had no hope of winning but I wanted to find out if there would ever be any hope for my type of writing – and used the pseudonym's anonymity to ensure an objective adjudication.

On the Tuesday of the crowning ceremony, I was sitting on the stage with the other members of the Bardic Circle, nervous and anxious to hear how the adjudicators would judge my entry. I comforted myself knowing I was the only one to recognise my nom de plume, which was 'Nebo', the name of a little mountain that my grandmother used to climb when she needed to boost her spirits. The adjudication was delivered by a well-known poet, Gwilym R. Jones. I was listening intently but it was very difficult to understand the speaker when sitting in the rows behind him. It is still difficult even today with all our new technology. I heard Gwilym R. Jones picking out, I think, five noms de plume, mine among them. I didn't hear his explanation but I took it for granted that he had decided that the ones he had named were not good enough to be in the competition. I was silently shattered, my worst thoughts having been confirmed. Not being able to confide in anybody, the eisteddfod dragged on. The Eisteddfod volume, with all the written adjudications, appeared on the Thursday after the chairing ceremony. As a rule, friends gathered to read and discuss. I bought my book, took it back to my hotel and packed it, without a glance, in my luggage. It was the following Wednesday, after I got home, that I plucked up the courage to read how badly I had been criticized by the adjudicators. I had to read what the adjudicator had said three times. I found it unbelievable. The five names he had mentioned were being praised for their efforts and I was being congratulated on my vers libre attempt. I began gaining confidence and forgot that I had decided never to compete again. It took me two years before I felt able to send my second entry to be judged. It was a metrical drama and I decided my theme would be Marie Antoinette. I didn't win but actually got a pat on the back from none other than that great man himself, Sir Thomas Parry.

That same year, browsing through the programme for Gŵyl Fawr Aberteifi, the annual Cardigan eisteddfod, my eye caught the subject for the Crown poem – *Mieri lle bu Mawredd* ('Briars where once there was greatness'). In my mind's eye, I saw my old friend Dewi Emrys standing before me. I felt I had to do something. I found I had two days to send in my attempt. Had my mother been alive, she would have been in agony visualising me working through the night. But sleep was not important. Here was a man whose grandeur of spirit had been lost in the wilderness of life. At the time I was struggling to fit the rebel into his biography, so it was a case of following his journey through life to the end.

Yma
rhwng Garn Gowil a'r môr bu bywyd yn fwrlwm
cyn i'r saint werthu eu ffermydd a'u heneidiau i'r Saeson.

Yr oedd cân yn y gwynt,
yr oedd anadl einioes yn yr hirnosau gwyllt.
Yr oedd mab y gweinidog yn cronni o athrylith.

Yn y dyddiau hynny
bu yma fawredd y gymdeithas werinol,
a gwylan yn dal y gwynt uwch cae gwenith.

Bu ffair a phregeth
yn siprys o fywyd yn y parthau hyn,
a dynion yn treulio'r blynyddoedd o stori i stori
cyn mynd o un i un i seleri'r achau
yn Rhos y Caerau, Pen Caer a Llanwnda.

Heddiw
mae'r chwyn pryfoclyd, y drain, y mieri a'r ysgall
dros lwybrau llencyndod y gŵr aflonydd
a bechodd yn anfaddeuol yn erbyn y Saint . . .

(Here
between Garn Gowil and the sea, life was healthily bubbling
before the saints sold their farms and their souls to the English.

There was a song in the wind.
There was a breath of life in the long, wild nights.
The Minister's son was a mass of ingenuity.

In those days
there was a majesty in the peasant community,
and the seagull caught the wind over a field of wheat.

A fair and a sermon
like a mixture of oats and barley, became the life of these areas,
and people spent their lives from story to story
before being carried one by one to the ancestral cellars
in Rhos y Caerau, Pen Caer and Llanwnda.

Today
the provoking weeds, the thorns, the briars and the thistles
have overtaken the childhood paths of the boy now a restless man
and judged to have sinned beyond forgiveness against the saints . . .)

It reached the secretary on the closing date under the nom de plume 'Rebel' in fond remembrance of a poet I deeply respected. I won the crown. I am sure Dewi Emrys, who had urged me so often to compete at the National Eisteddfod, would have been pleased. At the night of the crowning ceremony, I met the adjudicator for the first time, R. Bryn Williams, Camwy, Aberystwyth, that soft-voiced son of the Wladfa (Patagonia), later to become Archdruid of Wales. We became instant friends.

There used to be a saying that, if you won the Cardigan Gŵyl Fawr, you would go on to win the National Eisteddfod. I didn't believe that, but it did give me confidence to send in an entry in 1967. The subject that year was *Corlannau* ('Sheep folds'). I knew absolutely nothing about sheep. So that was that. Except that I couldn't quite get it out of my head. Aunty Hannah was rather poorly and I needed some activity to keep me going.

One night, in bed, things stirred in my head. I had recently been out in Morocco. It had been quite an experience. I had spent a lot of time in Marrakesh. I had a young guide, Hassan, son of Abdel Mahmoud, who took me to all the nooks and crannies of this fascinating Arab town. Mahmoud, a snake charmer, was the most innocent and sincere person I had ever met, and when Hassan had finally coaxed me to watch his father's dancing snake, we became friends. His wife had died about three years before and I was allowed to follow him to her grave where he talked to her as if she were still alive. He unloaded all his worries – when could his little girl wear high heels instead of sandals? When could Hassan have a new suit? Did he have to call with his mother-in-law every morning? It was tourist time and time was money . . . His wife was still there and approachable. I bought the Koran and found a whole new world to try to understand.

When I moved on to Rabat, Hassan brought me a farewell present from his father. It was a beautiful basket of intricate native weaving. I carried it proudly on my arm. When I spotted a seat, I went to sit for I was itching to see if the inside was as finely wrought as the outside. Even today, my knees still seem to turn to jelly when recalling that day and the shock. There it was, a sleeping snake, like a golden chain around one's neck. With a concentrated Olympian strength, I threw the basket and the snake into a purple profusion of bougainvilleas nearby and scuttled through a bundle of natives crouching on the edge of the kerb. Hassan followed bubbling with mischief. Even today with the distance of years, I still feel rather guilty. I tried to explain to the father of my sheer dread of being near to a snake. He had given me the most treasured snake in his possession – one that he had trained to dance to his mystic Arabic music. I don't think even his dead wife could make him understand that even if his snake danced like Margot Fonteyn, I would still be paralysed if left alone with one.

I moved on to the Atlas mountains. I read the Koran from cover to cover. I cannot pretend to understand the Islamic faith but I found the Koran fascinating. There were phrases that I did not comprehend but which were still music to the ear. I scribbled a poem in the vastness of quietude. Too often, my scribbling poems get lost but somehow this one saved itself. I had seen it when looking for something else. I got out of bed and went for it. I decided that I had found my 'folds'. Not ever competing for winning only, I recklessly thought, let those who know their sheep get on with it. My folds would be Islam, Christianity and Buddhism. I admit I should have given it more thought. I was censured by one or two critics for dealing with Buddhism after Christianity. I had a simple reason at the time. That great debater, T.E. Nicholas (Niclas y Glais) and I used to have friendly discussions at Aberystwyth and the topic as ever would be China. I was stuck with this fear of the Yellow Peril.

Today, with the inroads China is making to become a world power, my confusion is absolute. I don't know whether I regret winning the crown on such a theme or not. I certainly had not expected to win. And I still read the Koran at odd times.

I did what I could with my comparative-religions thought, and posted the poem under the nom de plume 'Glyn-y-Mêl', out of respect for my old friend Dewi Emrys. This was a long time before we built our bungalow and named it 'Glyn –y-Mêl' so no one would connect me with the entry. Posting was a relief. I didn't have a hope of winning. So that was that.

There came a night when I was the guardian angel sitting the whole night with Aunty Hannah. I had to keep awake for medicine times.

I found some paper to scribble on. Suddenly, I was in the throes of the folds of the life of Edith Piaf. I started at 11pm and finished at 3am. I knew the Eisteddfod entries had to be in the day after next. I had a little debate with myself. But why not? I typed it hurriedly not really being able to decipher chunks of my own writing. I put it in an envelope, mistakes and all, too overwhelmed to read it through. I added the sealed envelope, with my name and address, that would never be opened – unless I won. I knew there was no likelihood of that, but in case somebody sneaked to find out who had written this garbled entry, I gave my name as Adeline, a true one, but one I never used publicly, so I would remain unknown. I posted it the next day, and felt utterly ashamed of my effort. My nom de plume was 'Dans la peau' ('Under my skin'), very appropriate, but in the end I managed to blot it out until the crowning ceremony itself at Bala that August.

How can anyone but a topsy-turvy victim have so many muddled happenings in one life? It was nearing the first week in August.

I was hurriedly getting myself to go to Cardiff for two days. The postman delivered some letters. I glanced at them quickly. Opening one, I saw the heading *Eisteddfod Genedlaethol Cymru* ('The National Eisteddfod of Wales'). Ah well. Cardiff was calling. The Eisteddfod was always asking for money. I left it folded without reading it – and put it with the others in my desk to be seen to when I got back. I arrived back on the third day accompanied by an architect friend from Cardiff, Ron Wigley. He was going to design the bungalow we were always about to

156

build across the road from our old home. He had brought all the plans and we were in for a serious session.

At coffee break, I went to my desk to rifle through whatever correspondence needed to be seen to. This time I opened the folded Eisteddfod letter and read it properly. It was from Cynan, the Gorsedd Recorder at the time, informing me that I had won the Crown with the Glyn-y-Mêl entry. I have never passed out in my life. What kept me from doing so that time, I'll never know. I don't know exactly what I felt – disgust more than anything, maybe. How could I have so carelessly gone to Cardiff with a letter from Cynan, of all people, reaching me with such unexpected news? I went to tell my big sister, Get. We both knew that no one outside the family must know. Cynan had always been to me, the epitome of the Eisteddfod. In no way would I let him down. In any case, I was in too much awe of his disapproval. I went back to Ron, and what had been before, the exciting plans stretched out before us. I couldn't concentrate. After all I had never won a National Crown before. Ron knew there was something wrong and told me that he didn't think I had been listening to a word he had been saying. It was so true and he himself was such a true friend. My sudden decision won. I asked Ron whether he could keep a secret. He answered solemnly that he could, and would, if I really wanted to involve him. I told him and explained the top secrecy. I knew him, and had absolute trust in his promise. Bless him. He never did tell anyone. But, the day of the crowning ceremony, he rented a room in the Park Hotel, Cardiff and collected all my friends who used to gather when I was working at the BBC, Park Place, Cardiff, to view the ceremony on television. When he was asked how he had known in advance, his only answer was that he was psychic. I miss him. Cardiff has never been the same since we lost him.

The only thing that I dislike about winning top awards is the secrecy that has to be maintained before the event. It's killing. I became so paranoid that I became a prisoner in my home. Naturally I would have liked to have had my hair set as only my special hairdresser, Jackie of Cardigan, can do. She has attended to me in all my panics for almost half a century. If I need any questions answered, I go to her. If I'm commissioned to write something in a hurry and telephones ring, door bells clang and visitors can't read a 'Do not disturb, I'm working' sign, I always have an open-door haven in Jackie's Salon. She is a rare gem, difficult to find in these modern no-brake lives. I had another reason also, for avoiding her salon on this momentous occasion. I generally met Mair Garnon there, that capable Eisteddfod follower and outstanding orator. She has also been for years one of Jackie's faithful customers. A year after I won the Cardigan crown, I remember being in the salon just before going to the National Eisteddfod. Mair was there and asked me in her direct manner, if I was going to win the National crown that year. Luckily I could truthfully answer that time that I hadn't competed. So you see why it was that I had to go to Bala to have my crown fitted on top of a mop of hair which must have resembled a haycock in a hurricane!

Then I had to find someone I could rely on to get me to my feet when the Archdruid ordered me to stand up. I knew the very one. Lena Williams, Lampeter (or the objectionable Mrs Powell y Parke in the radio soap *Teulu'r Mans)*. We were great friends, and, having been driven there by another good friend, her husband Oliver, we arrived at the Maes about two hours before the ceremony. There was a decided reason for this. Every Eisteddfod, before I even thought of competing, a gang of us devoted *eisteddfodwyr* would play detectives to discover who was going to capture the Chair or the Crown. Our chief inspector was Peter Davies, Goginan, a veteran *eisteddfodwr* and competitor. We were generally looking for men – women were a rare breed in winning top prizes. If a man was dressed in a new suit, and wearing a Persil-clean shirt, and possibly had his family guarding his runaway tongue, he became our winner. Such detection was a highlight well up on our list of Eisteddfod duties. I used to get to the Eisteddfod for the first day and leave on the last each year. This year I knew I couldn't face Peter Goginan and his spies.

Lena and I stepped on the field. Almost the first person we saw was Peter Goginan. He shouted 'Congratulations, Luned.' I could have suffered a heart attack. If Peter knew, then the whole world around us knew. He would have been genuinely glad and anxious to broadcast my success. I was too dumb to say a word, not even 'Thank you'. I had visions of Cynan going for my jugular. I dragged Lena with me to the toilet. We stayed there for over an hour-and-a-half. Then we had to go in for the ceremony. I had been given two tickets so they could keep tabs on where I would be sitting, I guess. I gave them to Lena. In no way was I capable of doing anything right after the disaster. Lena got us to our seats. I was happy for the first time. My seat was right behind a pillar holding the building up. I could hide and had the pillar to hold on to when my legs would probably be buckling under. Lena was furious that they should have put me, the winner, behind a pillar.

I tried to calm her. One of the stewardesses saw Lena's uneasiness and came to investigate. We were, as it transpired, a long way from our proper seats. The lights had gone off for the televised crowning so we had to tread our way across legs and feet to reach our proper places. By now I was doubly nervous. Professor Alun Llywelyn Williams was giving the adjudication. He was mentioning 'Glyn-y-Mêl' and 'Dans la Peau' in his top class. He sounded as if he himself wanted to give the crown to the 'Dans la Peau' entry. I didn't hear any more. I become deaf if I am emotionally excited. I tried to remember how badly I had written the Piaf poem. Nothing made sense. Then the Archdruid was on his feet, asking 'Glyn-y-Mêl', and 'Glyn-y-Mêl' only to stand at the fanfare's call. With the help of Lena, I got up shakily. Immediately someone in a seat behind me pulled my skirt and told me in rather a threatening voice: 'Will you sit down. I want to see.' I was about to do so when I got 'Not on your life' from Lena, who held me standing in a firm grip. I turned round to apologise to the man behind. He just opened his mouth to give me a resounding 'No'. He told the people around that he had not expected a woman to stand up.

My day was far from at an end. I was taken by Cynan to the Eisteddfod bus to take off my crowning gown. I was then carried on the shoulders of some of the press men to be interviewed, with Cynan's voice shouting: 'You can't do this. Eluned is coming with us.' I was taken to a tent full of reporters. The London press were there for full coverage at that time. Later they stopped coming, because, I believe, most of the winners were not prepared to answer questions in the English language. I have always been against this as I think we should benefit from letting people who do not understand our language know what is going on in Wales, especially in cultural matters.

The press liaison officer, Clifford Phillips, welcomed me. Idris Roberts, BBC, asked his permission to have a short interview with me in Welsh before the London reporters took over. It was a live interview and to this day I have no recollection of what I said. This gentle-voiced Mr Phillips turned to me and asked if I would mind then answering a few questions in English. I thought he was pulling my leg so I answered very seriously, 'I think I did know a few words in English at one time, I will do my best'. I think one or two of the reporters who knew me burst into laughter. I explained to the nice Mr Phillips at the end that I gave him a flippant answer as I had gathered he was pulling my leg. He said he had been quite serious, explaining that the winners of Chairs and Crowns were mostly ministers and farmers and they always needed time to slip from one language to the other. I felt really ashamed and realised that I had a lot to learn about this competing business.

In the end I didn't leave the Maes until after 9 pm. There was a message from the *Liverpool Post*, asking if I would stay on the grounds to be available for an interview for their paper. They were sending a woman reporter since a woman had won the Crown. She eventually arrived. She had no knowledge of the Eisteddfod so I had to take her through the drill. There was a message also via the BBC that there was a crowd of about two to three hundred people on Lamb Square, Newcastle Emlyn waiting for my arrival home in Cenarth. When we eventually got out to the High Street at Bala, it was packed, and Lena, Oliver and myself were starving. We only managed to eat at one of the hotels because a policeman recognised that I had won the Crown in the afternoon.

We got to Lamb Square at 2 am! There was a wonderful cheering crowd there with the Rev. Clement Davies in charge. They had found a bardic chair and I sat on it and was taken down to Cenarth on a milk lorry, in pitch-black darkness with an escort of police officers. The drive to my home was festooned with flowers and balloons. It had all been done by the villagers. My big sister Get and Aunty Hannah in the house had been too busy to know, answering the telephone like robots, according to outsiders.

At 5 am I was on my way back to Bala to be interviewed by ITV for breakfast television. Still my worries did not end. I generally stay at hotels during the Eisteddfod week as being in and out for concerts, dramas, etc. would not be fair on private families. This time the Eisteddfod gave me the address of a private house, within a short distance of the Eisteddfod grounds. I was quite happy there. After the interview, I went back to the house. I found my bed had been taken by a very persistent David Lloyd, a tenor I adored. He wouldn't move. There was no way I would force my favourite tenor to move out for me, although I was in the right. I really didn't know what to do; every place seemed packed. I walked into the White Lion Hotel not really hoping there would be a spare bed. Cynan's sister Kerry was there. She shouted across and asked where I was staying. I began to tell her that as yet I didn't know but was saved by a strange lady saying 'She's staying with me'. Kerry gave a whoop of joy – 'Great. We are all staying there'. This Samaritan lady was a Mrs Johnson, who lived in a glorious mansion above Bala town. I have never been so feted in all my life.

Somebody arranged a celebration for the Thursday night. I have been to a few in my time, but never to one that lived up to this one. Mrs Johnson was an ex-ballet dancer but there was nothing ex about her. She, with a beautiful rose held by rosy lips, kicked the chandelier with the agility of a twenty-year-old. She had even commanded her daughter, a career ballet dancer, to come from London to dance at my celebration.

A gentleman I only knew as Goronwy, pressed a cheque into my hand – whispering 'for the drinks'. I thanked him for the fiver, which I thought was over-generous. Every one was so kind. Later I looked at the cheque. I was stunned. It wasn't for five pounds, but £250, a serious amount of money in 1967. I am a Cardi and about two whiskies a year is my limit. I wasn't certain I'd recognise the kind Goronwy again. But I couldn't accept that amount of money for the party drinks. I found Cynan and told him my objection. He told me Goronwy was a friend of his and could well afford it – I think he owned a caravan site or something. I was still unhappy, and since Goronwy didn't seem to be around, I passed the onus of sorting it out to Cynan. I only know it turned out to be a glorious celebration. I wanted to help with the party preparations. They appointed me to be the cucumber slicer. I happily threw my energy into it. My mind was overloaded with the events of the week. I ended up with a cucumber heap the size of Snowdon. I'll never forget that extravagance. Even today, some of the people present that night still shout 'Cucumbers!' whenever they see me. Mrs Johnson became a friend for life.

With the publication of the volume of winning entries and written adjudications on the Thursday, I had a post mortem to face on the Friday! I bought the book and tried to secure a quiet spot on the Maes to find out what the judges had said about my entries. I was actually approached by Alun Llywelyn Williams after the ceremony, who confirmed that he himself would have chosen the Piaf one for the crown. I think it was the vicar on the panel who prevented that happening. And who can really blame him? But didn't my grandmother say that we should know a person personally before ever delivering judgment.

The Second Crown

I did not compete again until the 1980s. What with travelling, family illnesses and building a bungalow, there was no time for creative thinking. But in Llangefni in 1983, I won my second National Crown, though once again, things had not been straightforward. In fact, I nearly lost out on sending in an entry. It was that topsy-turvy streak playing up again. Let me try to explain.

During the 1982 Swansea and District National Eisteddfod, I was staying at the Dragon Hotel, Swansea. One afternoon, I'd arranged to have my annual battery-charging session with those two eisteddfodic medics and cultural experts, Dr John Owen, Porthcawl, and the North Walian wonder surgeon, Owen Owen, Bangor. We also had a well known singer from Covent Garden whose name is playing hide-and-seek with my tired memory at the moment. We were in for a wealth of wisdom. Owen Owen took centre stage. He started by taking us back to the origins of the Celts. I was listening, most probably with my mouth wide open, and certainly with eyes like over-sized saucers. I have always been proud to proclaim myself a Celt. It's unbelievable, but I must stress that I listened without interrupting for surely almost three hours. Absolutely fascinating stuff. I had Dr John the other side of me. Fair play, in the Celtic excitement we hadn't been too fair to him. He, too, was such a brilliant speaker. I turned to him and as it was the Falklands War year, we plunged into a deep debate. The Celts and the Falklands war were equally important to me. A young soldier from Llechryd, the next village to mine, had been killed out there on the Sir Galahad. His grandfather was the quick-witted man who had saved me from choking in that cask of black tar. I promised Dr

John before leaving that I would write a play setting out my troubled thoughts.

The subject for the1983 Llangefni Eisteddfod *pryddest* (a poem not in strict metre) was *Clymau* ('Bonds' or 'Ties'). I knew immediately that I was going to have a go. I had Owen Owen's Celts buzzing around my head. It must be the Bonds of the Celts. I bought about twenty books on the Celts and studied them avidly. About three weeks before the deadline, I sat down with paper and pen at the ready. I was confident of inspiration. I struggled in the late hours, bruised and battered. I thought back to the old plagues, the Black Death, leprosy. I had a new disease, the Celtic plague. My feverish head was overloaded. I was faced with at least eight poems. There was no way I could whip them into one sensible poem for a competition. I had been over-confident and was beaten. Unusually for me, I had thought it all out. I had planned to fit my poem into the old Celtic form of composition, but without adopting the *cynghanedd* used in the Chair competition today. But, for days and nights on end, I groaned inwardly and silently for my lost cause.

Then, tossing and turning in bed one night, I found myself harking back to that afternoon in the Dragon Hotel and my conversation with Dr John. I had promised to write a powerful drama about the Falklands war. I saw it in a flash. The bond between those Welsh boys out in the Falklands who were fighting Argentinian boys of Welsh blood, the descendants of the people from Wales who had gone out on the Mimosa in 1865 to form a new Welsh colony in Patagonia. I had about a week to get this long poem going. Without much thought, I used the form I had intended for the Celtic marathon.

After I had posted my entry, I realised that one of the adjudicators was James Nicholas, a very able strict-metre man, who was also a mathematician: he, surely, would not condone my abandonement of the clicking consonants that are the trademark of traditional strict-metre poetry. I accepted that my chances of winning were nil. I had been taught by my mother never to bear a grudge at losing, whether I was reciting or writing.

I was pleased at having done my best to set out my thoughts about the Falklands war. I forgot the effort and settled back into normal civilian life. I certainly didn't make myself ill waiting for the postman to deliver tidings of great joy, as I am told some keen competitors are inclined to do a week or so before the eisteddfod.

I did not receive a letter before the Llangefni National Eisteddfod, but I did receive a telephone call. That faithful friend, Alun Tegryn Davies, asked me to meet him at the entrance of the old grammar school in Cardigan. I admit I have never been well up on eisteddfodic manoeuvres, and being the only woman apart from the Mistress of the Robes, at committee meetings, I felt on the fringe of events. But Alun Tegryn was one of my trusted friends. He was the Gorsedd's Acting Recorder at the time and he told me that he hadn't wanted to call at my home because eisteddfodic spies are clever at putting two and two together, so he was personally bringing me the news that I had won the Crown at Llangefni. The impossible does happen, after all, I thought. We drove around the lonely back lanes of Gwbert, while he gave me the drill of utter secrecy for the forthcoming eisteddfod. After the shock that the Falklands poem had been accepted, non-clicking consonants and all, I thoroughly enjoyed our Scarlet Pimpernel escapade.

The second time round can never really be as exciting as the first. But the fact that I wanted the world to know my feelings about the Falklands war helped to maintain the momentum.

But I had learnt my lesson. I was prepared for the detectives this time. If someone congratulated me on the Maes before the ceremony this time, I would stop and talk to them. I had never lived down the fact that I had dragged my friend Lena to hide with me in the toilet for an hour-and-a-half after Peter Goginan shouted 'Congratulations' at Bala! Had I stopped to talk to Peter at the time, I would not have worried myself sick thinking that the whole of Wales knew I was to be the winner. When I did speak to him after the ceremony, I found out that he didn't have a clue that the Crown was to be mine. He was congratulating me on a radio programme I had broadcast just before arriving at the eisteddfod! I put it down, as usual, to my red genes tangoing out of control.

I managed at Llangefni without any outsized mishaps. I had my nephew Stephen and his wife Yvonne in control. There was one hiccup that might have turned into an embarrassment. After the ceremony, T. Glynne Davies, the Llanrwst poet, appointed himself my escort to guide me through the crowds on the Maes to meet the Press who that year were waiting cosily in the HTV establishment. It took us almost two hours to cross the field. T. Glynne, with the patience of a saint, carrying my crown, would sit it on my head when various members of the public wanted to take photographs, and there seemed to have been about two hundred Americans on the Maes that afternoon. I don't remember who the MC at HTV was that afternoon. But I do remember that dear, ever-courteous friend, David Meredith, asking if he could introduce me, since we had been acquainted for some time. He was given instant permission and his charming words of praise made me tingle with pride. He knew of my willingness always to talk to those reporters who weren't Welsh speaking, so he finished with a flourish and told the audience 'And now Eluned is prepared to talk to you in any language.' Oops! The roots of my red hair were glaring through the grey. Was there someone from China, from Russia, from Pakistan, among those about to embarrass me? For once my red gremlins were on holiday. I survived.

Llangefni closed one chapter of my life. There would be no more competing. I had won two National Crowns and was thus debarred from entering again. I suppose I could have set my sights on the National Chair. I had, after all, been taught *cynghanedd* when I was quite young, but I am not a natural user of this strict metre, unlike Dic Jones, Gerallt Lloyd Owen, Alan

Llwyd and that charming and talented Mererid Hopwood, among many others, of course. It would take me a long time to write a long poem for the Chair, and long drawn-out matters and I are not the best bedmates.

Indeed, if the truth be told, thanks to my American adventures, I have become used to a more instantaneous method of writing because their composers usually need their words a week before, and sometimes even a fortnight before they have even asked for them! Such things keep me on my antique toes.

Another Peep at my Village

Before telling you about my American adventures, I would like you to have another little peep at the village and area that has moulded my ninety years plus. I wrote a Welsh poem once, '*Fy Etifeddiaeth*', crystallizing my feelings. Here is a typically inadequate translation.

My Heritage

Black coracles ago
There was a flurry of excitement
on the banks of the Teifi at the coming of Spring
and the season of salmon with the thrill of the 'catch'
after the mean lean-ness of the winter.
A sense of hope followed the close guarding of the river
from the poaching spooks of darkness.

Here
the whiteness of the flowering blackthorn,
and the dancing foam of the Falls were pure
as the virgin's dress before the Altar of union
and the only law was the law of the Commune.

A neighbour was a neighbour
straddling rustically over the threshold to hearth,
before polite knocking on doors,
plastered its hoary frost to spike the welcome.

The village sage huddled on the settle
under the old open chimney where a salmon hung smoking,
and busy hands knotted nets to caress a meagre living.

Arguments were fiery around Simon Peter and John,
 and Christ Jesus, the Master, on the strike down the river,
 the eyes of the debaters never wavering from the path
 of Daniel Tŷ Oli's tobacco spit aimed towards the fireplace,
 lest it extinguish the tongue of the flame.
 Ever present, the imploring fingers of Ann Gof
 coaxing a nappy to protect her eleventh,
 before hands were disciplined to pluck
 the Welfare State bald.

Today, the armada of coracles has disappeared
under the tyranny of the law,
and that old fox, Death, has mangled
one by one, the keepers of our heritage,
and forced the lone partner
to allow the last coracle to be battered
by the flood of hiraeth
on its way to the sea.

But the flurry of excitement remains
on the banks of the Teifi.
The favoured rich come to toast their 'catches'
on expensive stretches of water.

Prisoners from cities gather
from local summer homes,
 their eyes full of wonder to stare
at the water, and to look long at the whiteness
of the Falls, and the white buds
of the blackthorn.

Above the prattle of the Falls,
the know-all scientist proclaims
that the whiteness is the same as the white
seen on the crown of thorns
on a Cross long ago.

Yes. The old days. In Cenarth today, I doubt whether there remain as many as four families of the ones I knew when I was young. Am I sentimental? I don't think so. I never mind moving on. I count my blessings that at my age, I still have friends around if I need them. I peep from my window in my little pink bungalow at Howell's bungalow across the river. I've known him all my life. He is the son of Johnny Jones, Argoed, that charismatic and generous man who was chair when I was running the village activities during the war. Tim and Hetty Jones live not far away and keep a keen eye on my movements. Tim, as a young boy, looked after the fire in the hall where we fought sometimes to have our Welcome Home concerts. His brother Ken, you may remember was the one I recklessly kept in the village to act in a play, probably denting the war effort. Now up the road from me I have Rhiannon and Jeff Lewis. A delightful pair, both now retired, but still as busy as ever. Rhiannon was the music mistress at Ysgol y Preseli, the Welsh-medium comprehensive school in Crymych, north Pembroke-shire. She has helped me out when I need a music expert to sort out a hurried, complex command from that genius of a composer Michael J. Lewis, Los Angeles (more of him in my next chapter.) She is the chattiest, most fun person, I know and a tonic to visit you if you are in pain. Jeff, I have known all my life. His parents lived on the square at Cenarth. He has recently retired from being headmaster of Ysgol y Ddwylan, the primary school in Newcastle Emlyn. It is a bonus to have them living nearby. Mrs Enid Faccio lives down the road from me. She married an Italian ex-prisoner of war, and is the daughter of the Hannah Sexton I used to write and sing verses about in our concerts. Not blessed with a lot of worldly goods, she was the most generous-hearted, happy person I knew. Then there is June Gray, who, though she lives in Aberporth, picks me up every Sunday to go to the same chapel that I attended in those far-off childhood days.

I must also introduce you to my Man Friday. Andrew

Gilbert, a born-and-bred Cardiffian who has come west with his partner, Netta, and his two young boys Jordan and Ashley. He was a top restaurateur in Cardiff for years, but as well as being a chef and wine connoisseur, he can play the parts of an escort, a chauffeur, a painter and decorator and a very judicious editor of scripts, et al. He is no mean raconteur, either. Since I was a passenger in two serious car crashes in 1997, and am no longer allowed to lift heavy weights, he is also my chief Samaritan and takes me shopping. He even drove me to Heathrow for my flight to Los Angeles.

And that reminds me of another great friend who has for years helped me on my way to Heathrow, Councillor David Snook of Llanharri, near Cardiff, whose collection of hats is well known in Cenarth. He and his lovely wife, Hilary, have been friends of mine for years and come fishing in the area. Through them I have another charming friend in Llanharry, Sibyl Jones. She and her son Gareth breed pedigree, prize-winning dogs.

Thanks to their kindness, the Snooks and I have a well-established Heathrow routine. When I go to Los Angeles, twice and sometimes, three times a year, David arrives at my home the day before. I stay with them the night, then however early I need to get to the airport, David takes me to Bridgend to board the National Express that deposits me in Terminal Three at Heathrow. And knowing now that I am truly a topsy-turvy person, you can imagine that the journeys have had more than a few hiccups. I will just give you one instance. One morning I had to catch the 4am coach at Bridgend. No problem there. David had been taking me to the bus station there for quite a number of years. We arrived at the usual place in good time. But where was the bus station? I thought I must be asleep. There was no way that David had lost his way. David knew the place blindfolded and Hilary, a night nurse at the local hospital, drove into the town each night. But we were facing a blank space. How could someone steal a whole bus station? There was no one around to ask at that unearthly hour. I saw a bus in the distance and asked David whether it was coming our way. I won't repeat the expletive that fell from his lips – it was so totally unusual. I didn't have time to think of anything to say as he bundled me back into the car and I understood that we would be racing to catch the coach at Cardiff. Full marks to my friend David. We did it. We yelled at the people at the bus stop not to let the Express go without me. I still remember that journey. I saw a sunrise somewhere beyond Chepstow that beat an unbeatable one I once saw in South Africa. That blotted out the mystery of the missing bus station. I don't like unsolved mysteries but when I got to the plane, I felt as happy as Miss Marple. A lovely stewardess, came to see if I was comfortable. She had a wholesome Welsh accent. I asked from where. She answered sweetly 'Bridgend.' I told her I hadn't really wanted to be reminded of Bridgend. She sympathised with my treatment by the Express coach. They had decided that they needed a new modern depot and had removed the pick-up point to outside the Spar shop in town. Now can you see the logic in that? I couldn't. Without someone telling me, I never do my shopping in Spar at the crack of dawn.

I may as well add the other bit. I feel calmer now. I telephoned David and Hilary from Los Angeles to tell them the new pick-up point was outside Spar. David said he'd be right there to pick me up on my return in about a month. He was there. The bus stand wasn't. National Express management had moved their coaches to another stand, miles away. The bus drivers thought they could leave me at their new stand. They could think otherwise. That night I was almost glad to be a redhead. I was sorry for the other passengers on board but I felt that I had to take control and they all had to be bussed with me and my luggage to where my reliable friend David stood patiently waiting for the bus to arrive. Thinking it over in quiet Cenarth, I can only put it down to this modern texting – people don't seem to know how to communicate with common sense any more.

Cenarth has always been, and still is, a paradise for anglers. The most avid rod-and-line angler, even if he does not catch a sewin or salmon bigger than his outstretched arms, has the bonus of the beauty of the Teifi valley all around. The mode of fishing has altered with the years. When I was young, I remember about seventeen pairs of coraclemen trawling down the river, each pair dragging a net between them. It was a family livelihood. They were a jolly lot. I can still see in my mind's eye one character, Johnny Morgan Rees, who used to live in the cottage near Salmon Leap, putting his coracle down after coming back from his 'strict' (the distance they fished down the river) in the centre of the village square, running into the White Hart pub for a few pints, and coming out singing heartily and doing a clog dance around the coracle! Anyone present would throw a coin into his nearby up-turned cap. I remember old Daniel Williams in his old age too, managing the old traditional dance, after a hefty catch. It was a meagre living, but a happy one. It was a sad day when a bye-law put a stop to coracle fishing.

And this is where, I think, I should make a confession to ease my conscience. Not being a Catholic, I have never been absolved. In my young days, when living at Glanawmor across the road, our land went right down to the Teifi. Our little stream ran into the Teifi. That is where my old home got its name, it seems, according to Aneirin Talfan Davies. He explained to me that the inspection ships used to come up from the port at Cardigan to the point where the little stream entered the big river, hence *Glan-naw-môr* ('the banks of the nine seas'). I disputed that, too. I had always thought the old saying evoked the 'seven' seas. But I had a lot of respect for scholarly Aneirin Talfan and certainly accepted his explanation.

My mother's cousin lived in Tegfan, the bungalow across the road to us. He had a son Cyril, softly spoken and soft footed. Ideal for a poacher. In my younger days, poaching was a fun thing. An adventure. One or two of the village boys were a dab hand at it. And to be fair, I knew from one or two in the village that if someone was ill, a slice or two of salmon or sewin on the menu would be more of a tonic than a whole bottle of doctor's medicine. Call me a busybody. It's quite true, I like to be in on everything. The thought of being out under the stars and moon at about three or four in the morning in the quietude of my lovely valley was a temptation not to be resisted. I coaxed Cyril to let me be in on a poaching spree. I soon found I had a lot to learn. A poacher's night is a totally black one. However attractive I might have looked under the soft rays of a moon, the bailiffs would only see me as a thief. I took that to heart and wrote a sonnet in Welsh '*Y Potsier*' in an attempt to distance the poacher from an uncaring thief. I'll try to give you an English version:

The Poacher

He crept on the Teifi bank through the bracken,
his eyes like an ox in the twilight haze;
heading for the pool of his lucky omen,
slithering like a ghost through the thorny maze.
A Robin Hood on a night of adventure,
pouncing with glee on the silvery prize,
fondling his catch, a lad of nature,
hiding it slyly from forbidden eyes.
A triumphant return through the coves of witches
to a welcome 'come in' from one who was ill,
and the lights in the eyes of old Martha were riches
to last a lifetime for his hour of thrill.

Before the greed of the commercial murderer
destroyed the innocent joy of the old time poacher

Please, can I at least be half absolved for my confession? When the greedy professionals took over, I, and one or two others who had enjoyed poaching probably only twice a year, gave up entirely. The thrill had gone forever.

But before I finish with these fishy tales, I feel I must brag about one catch, which no elasticated stretching of arms, could ever encompass. This was definitely the one that did not get away.

Our National Eisteddfod of Wales Gorsedd (Bardic Circle) has for years had a link with the Breton Gorsedd. The Breton *Bardd Mawr* (equivalent to our Archdruid) would attend our ceremony bringing the Breton half of the sword of peace to be united with the Welsh one. I had known the *Bardd Mawr* Pierre Loisel for years: he would come and stay at my home and we'd travel together to wherever the National Eisteddfod was held that year. A few years ago, he had been at my home one Sunday night before moving on to, I believe, Llanrwst on the Monday. Cyril, my co-poacher at times, had come across to visit. The talk turned to poaching. Pierre became very excited and wanted to know how it was done. Cyril, who would use any excuse to go poaching, offered to show him that night. I tried to dissuade them, not because I was against going poaching that night, but because Pierre was short sighted, well actually extremely short-sighted – I think everybody who remembers him would agree – not wearing treble but double-treble lens. The two men insisted they would be alright so off we went.

It was a fairly dark night. In a way we were lucky. A tree from the wooded bank had fallen into the river, so our night was easier than usual. We would straggle along the tree trunk into the river and with any luck dip a net and catch a salmon. Things were going well until a stray briar caught Pierre's spectacles and flicked them into the water. Poor Pierre was blind without them so in trying to rescue them, he also fell in the river. Now we certainly had a weighty problem. Our *Bardd Mawr* was by no means a slim person. Cyril and I had had struggles before in netting heavy fish, but nothing like this helpless one. We did get him in the end and took him, half drowned, back to the house. And then there was a problem. This Breton was a stickler for dress code. Because it was a Sunday, he had his only white shirt on, the one he would need for the Monday's Eisteddfod ceremony. That was entirely non-negotiable. A guest is a guest so I offered to wash the offending shirt. I'd never washed a man's shirt but I knew I had to add starch. The shirt luckily came out white enough but it could stand on its own. It was by this time after 4am. I crept sheepishly upstairs and went to my mother for advice. I had to re-wash the shirt and add the requisite amount of starch. We got to the Eisteddfod and no one was any the wiser. But believe me, I have boasted many times after, of that big fish I caught on a night of poaching.

To end this chapter, I think I must quote a memorable *englyn* (a strict-metre stanza) by Dewi Emrys, if my own ancient memory can remember – and translate – it properly:

> Ym merw byd y mae awr ber – i wyliwr,
> > Awr chwalu trais Amser;
> > Awr o swyn pan losgo'r ser
> > Edefyn y cnawd ofer.

> (In a bustling world, there's a sweet hour – to a spectator,
> > The hour that demolishes the rape of Time.
> > An hour of charm when the stars burn
> > The thread of all wasteful flesh.)

I will now, if I don't waylay myself again, concentrate on ending this marathon of my life journey. The following chapter should really not have happened but it has, and, once again, the unusual becomes the usual in my life. I admit I was rattled at the beginning when I was branded a topsy-turvy human being, but now that my red hair has turned grey, I agree and forgive.

America

I never ever wanted to set foot in America. My antipathy to the USA started subconsciously when I was staying at a London hotel, where a very fashionable and talkative American lady was also resident. She was from Colorado. I said I was from Wales. She had never heard of the place. I pointed out, reasonably enough, that it was a country, not a place. She was probably wondering whether I was geographically ignorant or economical with the truth. I took her home with me for three weeks. I convinced her of our Saint David's wisdom – little things are worth preserving. I had been wrong, too, in misjudging her country. Not all Americans are oversized, no more than their vehicles, buildings and opinions. In fact, I have found working in this fairly new country a breath of fresh air.

It was my friend Eira, bless her, who finally got my feet on American soil. She had a family wedding in Palos Verdes, California, and didn't fancy doing that very long trip on her own. We were ideal fellow travellers – the happy-go-lucky, no-grumbles kind. But I really did not want to go to America. Apart from the Colorado person I had kidnapped, I only knew one person in the whole country, Mary Lloyd Evans, and she lived on the Pacific Coast, almost a hundred miles from the Los Angeles airport! But I couldn't let Eira go on her own. And thus, the whole trip became an adventure, not a problem.

Eira was collected by her family. I wended my way out of the airport, charged with getting to Port Huenini, somewhere beyond Oxnard, Ventura. I passed through Arrivals knowing that there was no one there for me. Two strange ladies were, however, holding up a piece of paper with 'Eluned Phillips' written on it. Goodness me, another Eluned Phillips: the Welsh are everywhere, I thought.

177

On I went. Then felt a tap on my shoulder. A soft, kind voice asked if I was Eluned Phillips. I said I was but not the one they were looking for, as I had not expected to be met at the airport. It turned out that my friend Mary had telephoned the Clerk of the Sessions at the Welsh Church, the only one in Los Angeles. The Clerk at the time was David Evans (soon to become Dafydd Evans to me) and it was he who had sent the two 'strange' ladies to meet me! They were his wife, Olive, who had brought with her a friend, Gill Cole. It was a lovely thought. I was asked what I wanted to do. I said, I would like to have a proper cup of tea!

Going upstairs to the restaurant, I was stopped by one of the customs officers. (Have you noticed that they are always big, imposing men, so as to deflate your confidence?) I knew I wasn't carrying anything illegal but I was very, very bothered that these two kind ladies would be affronted by my packing, which always makes my suitcase look worse than a linen basket full of crumpled clothing. When I'm ashamed I always look down at my feet. Getting a little impatient, I asked the man 'What are you looking for?' The answer was, literally, deadly, and in a decisive voice it came: 'A hand grenade.' I'm surprised that my two-lady reception committe did not pass out. Did they now think they were aiding and abetting a terrorist? I stood there like a nitwit and wished that I was prone to passing out at such moments. My inquisitor was relentless. In the rubble, he found my toilet bag, held it up and asked 'What is this?' I peeped and, in front of these two fashionable ladies, was relieved it was not my old, tired and tattered one. With my reckless genes playing up again, I decided that I had to be bold to get by these men, so I answered him in my grandmother's no-nonsense fashion: 'You are holding up my toilet bag.' When he asked what was in it, I performed an angry somersault and came up with ' the normal things'. He opened it and found his hand grenade: an innocent, if obese, bottle of moisturising oil for my redhead's delicate skin. The by-now deflated official showed it to me on the scanning screen. Not ever having known a hand grenade, I accepted it did look suspicious so I turned my anger against those en route who had not spotted the calamity that did not happen. The giggles we had at the big man's expense made the two ladies, Olive Evans, Gill Cole and myself friends for life.

I had a wonderful time at the condominium with Mary and her cat. Poor Mary, however, had to answer a lot of telephone calls from friends telling her that they had seen me on television. I knew this was ridiculous. I hadn't seen even the ghost of a TV crew on my journey. Had I landed in the midst of people who believed in fairies – or maybe worse? One friend told Mary sharply, 'If you don't believe me come over, I've taped it'. I became more concerned. I must have a lookalike. My only consolation was that she would probably be a wiser character. It turned out that it was me, after all – but in a repeat, a programme I had been in about two years earlier when a producer from New York came to my house to interview me for a series they called 'The Story of English'. Though I'd agreed to take part at the time, when I realised they would edit the interview in such a way that would suggest that the English language was older than Welsh, there was no way that my red hair would countenance it. I told the pint-at-a-time beer swigger that in no way would I be a part of such traitorous attacks. Poor Wales has all too easily been trampled on through the ages. I stood adamant. I can hear her now, shouting as she drove down the drive: 'I'll get you in America yet'. I waved a fond farewell and erased it from my memory. She probably thought she had won the battle but she only won a small part of the battle by resurrecting a small part of the interview. Then I went to Canada the following year and found it was running, there, too. Like the body in the bag, it seems to follow me everywhere.

In the morning Mary went to work. I was quite happy meddling around and found myself standing outside a car port. There was a motorcycle, and a rather distinctive automobile or truck or whatever they call these expensive vehicles in which the wealthy drive around California. A gentleman came to say hello. He was Walter, Mary's neighbour, and he had carried in my luggage the night before. He told me that he was taking me to lunch since Mary was working. I thanked him and asked when he wanted to go. He said if I was ready we could go immediately. I thought he was a busy man and didn't want to waste his time so I jumped on the pillion of the motorbike. He smiled and said he was not taking a guest from Wales to lunch on a motorbike pillion and opened the door of this posh truck.

I found out later that he owned a yacht, too. Appearances are always deceptive to a country girl like myself. Walter turned out to be a very interesting person. He was a high-up officer at the nearby Oxnard Naval Depot and one of the many extraordinarily kind Californians I have had the pleasure of meeting along the years. He took me all round Ventura, out in a boat on the Pacific, introduced me to my first chicken-in-the-basket and through him I met that wonderful writer, Garrison Keillor. He has written a number of books for adults and children, and poetry, too. I often listen to him on American radio. His style is so laid back that he could easily hypnotise you to sleep if you weren't afraid of missing one word of his interesting talks. Someone described him as having a 'down-comforter voice'. I'm charmed with his cosy story-telling. I once read a verse of his which went something like this –

> I can't stay, you know, I left so long ago.
> I'm just a stranger with memories of people I knew here.
> We stand around, looking at the ground.
> You're the stories I've told for years and years.

As I try to write these memoirs, I can relate to that verse – if only I had Keillor's captivating style.

I had press interviews. I was invited to read my poetry at various venues. One night I was reading at the house of a doctor friend of Mary's. The doctor's wife, Valerie, was an artistic weaver of prayer mats for mission halls, so the following morning she took me to several of these halls to see her work. They were absolutely gorgeous. The last mission hall on our list was at the top of Santa Barbara, a huge building surrounded by wild countryside. We are not strong on mission halls in Wales, and I needed a breath of fresh air. I saw a small wicket gate leading into scrubland beyond and I decided to take a walk along the track. I opened the gate and started walking. Someone shouted 'Mind the rattlesnakes.' Then I heard the rattle and saw the snake. I jumped back. I almost get paralytic even seeing the picture of a snake in a book. Valerie assessed my nervous state and said she was taking me down to Santa Barbara to the best native Mexican restaurant not only in the city but in the whole of America. I couldn't have cared less if it had been a MacDonalds; I merely wanted the greatest distance possible between me and that unmusical rattlesnake.

Valerie was well known to the proprietor of the restaurant for we got a table immediately. I was glad to sit down. We were given rather big glasses, rims salted, with large drinks. I saw Valerie lifting hers to drink, so being extra thirsty because of my snake experience, I gulped mine down in one go. I felt a red-hot poker whirling from the sole of my foot to the top of my head. Once all the liquid had trickled down my throat, I began smiling, like a Cheshire cat, at everyone in the room and beyond because the room had now extended itself to double size. I was happy, and everybody seemed to be happy for me. Valerie had told the proprietor that I was visiting from Wales. I never found out whether that was because she wanted everyone to know that this smiling cat was definitely not of American origin. The waiters brought me a taste of the various items on the menu. I came away with a bag full of memorabilia – pencils, notebooks, Mexican souvenirs – it was like a hundred Christmases rolled into one. That night, stretched on the floor of my friend's house, I spent hours instructing all around me how to make old-fashioned Welsh patchwork-quilts. Unfortunately, I had never in my life managed to sew even a patch on a much needed pair of jeans. I confess I was totally drunk, for the first and only time in my life. I discovered afterwards that I had drunk raw Mexican whiskey and tequila. From that following morning, I understood why those old, good-living preachers were constantly warning us about that sly serpent in the garden of Eden.

Having arranged originally to return home with Eira after a fortnight, it was five weeks before I actually got back to Cenarth! I blame the delay on the hospitality of Dafydd and Olivia Evans at Manhattan Beach, a place that has subsequently become my second home, and the second home of many indeed. The place is always bustling with interesting people, anyone visiting from Wales, England, Australia or wherever; students of all nationalities, especially musical ones. Dafydd himself is a trained tenor, and Olive, a writer, a brilliant story-teller, who has already published a book of teddy-bear poems, illustrated by a friend, Pat, originally from France, and together they are about to publish a follow-up collection.

At their table last year I was fortunate to meet Georgi Slavchev, young, talented and already a doctor of music, who is a composer full of inspiring enthusiasm: a likeable workaholic and total fun as well. There was an instant empathy. He had heard that I wanted to stage a musical, *Princess Nest* and asked if he could see a copy. When he saw the libretto, he knew it was a project for the future for he still had exams to conquer. He then saw the poem 'True Love', fell in love with the words and asked if he could compose music for it. He soon had a melody going but did not like the first singer who sang it. He did not give up and altered it to include a cellist. I couldn't be in Los Angeles for the concert but I hear it was sung to acclaim by a lovely Welsh soprano, Rachel Schutz, at the Singing Festival at the Welsh Presbyterian Church in Los Angeles. She lives with her parents in Germany, but is at the moment in a New York music college and has won numerous trophies including the under 25 years Blue Riband at the Welsh National Eisteddfod. She has a great future.

Another I met at Manhattan Beach was Sebastian Koch, a brilliant pianist from Paris, who has been the organist at the Welsh church in Los Angeles for years. Last time we were having a meal at Dafydd and Olive's, he ate a whole chicken by himself! Such is the Evanses' generosity.

I naturally go to the Welsh church as often as I can when I'm over in California. It is a delight always to meet the church's secretary, Evelyn Hughes, with her tranquil faith and warm welcome, is a sure comfort for someone who is 6,000 miles away from home. There also I meet quite often the Rev. I.D.E. Thomas, a born-and-bred Cardiganshire man, who is still very well known in Wales. Another fellow *Cardi* that I did eventually meet at the Welsh church was Michael J. Lewis of Penparcau, Aberystwyth, originally. I say 'eventually' with good reason.

This composer and conductor – critically acclaimed especially for his scores for films like *Julius Caesar* (starring John Gielgud), *The Madwoman of Chaillot* (starring Katherine Hepburn and Danny Kaye), and *The Medusa Touch* (starring Richard Burton) – actually sent me a letter and enclosed a disc of his film overtures. Now, I have always answered all correspondence whether I am interested or not but this was 1997, the year I was involved in two car crashes. In seemingly permanent convalescence, I neglected to answer the famous composer.

A few months later I was at the Welsh church. The music from the piano was melodiously enticing. I could only see the back of the pianist, broad-shouldered and tall. I asked who was playing. They told me. It was Michael J. Lewis, the man I had discourteously never answered. I would apologise at the gathering later. However, there were two biggish men there that day and, as you've come to expect, no doubt, I picked the wrong man. We had quite a laugh over my mistake. Michael came over to join in the fun. I tried again. My apology was accepted. We talked, we were, after all fellow Cardis, although Michael since his early years had been working in London and then Los Angeles. Michael said he was going to Wales the next day. I said I was also going home that day. He said he had a concert in Llanbadarn Fawr, Aberystwyth, on the Friday night and added abruptly, 'Be there.' Now nobody orders a redhead to do anything in that tone of voice. I answered vaguely, saying that if my diary was clear for the night, I might attend. I really was beginning to be hooked, however. I was free and turned up at the concert. After the very successful concert, I was totally hooked.

The following day the *cerdd dant* musicians were holding their harp competitions at the town's university hall. Michael asked if I would meet him there. I had intended spending a short time there anyway. We made an appointment to meet at 10am. I was there on time but there was no sign of Michael. After a while, I asked the president, whom I knew, whether he had seen Michael J. Lewis around. Yes, he had been there earlier. I decided to leave since I had told him I was only there for a short time. I had reached the exit, when Michael came thundering in. He apologised. He had been called unexpectedly down town. He bought me coffee and we sat at a table. Then he commanded curtly 'Show me your work.' I told him I didn't carry my work around with me. But he was like a rottweiler with a juicy bone. 'Can't you remember something?' I don't take kindly to being forced into doing anything and was about to thank him for the coffee and leave, when it flashed across my mind that there was a little poem I had written for Edith Piaf. But could I remember it? He found me pencil and paper, and stood over me. My handwriting is illegible, even to me, at the best of times, so how Michael ever managed to read the crow's feet I shall never know.

I went home from Aberystwyth. Michael was going back to Los Angeles next day. Two days later, I had a telephone call. The abrupt voice told me 'Sit down, and listen'. I sat down,

184

which I am glad I did. This sweet soprano voice wafting over the wires was taking my breath away. Michael's melody for 'Llwyd Bach y Baw' was so beautiful and the singer Caryl Ebenezer (an Aberystwyth girl) had the ideal voice to sing it. That started a worthwhile partnership with Michael which went on for years.

Writing lyrics for Michael has never been a problem. I enjoy the confidence that comes from knowing that the music will complement the words so perfectly. I can think of one in particular that has been quite a hit: 'True Love'. I have heard it sung as a duet by two first-class Welsh singers, and by two first-class Korean singers. And, just like Georgi Slavchev's setting of the same piece, it was truly beautiful. It has been sung all over California at weddings and anniversaries. Scripted on parchment and framed, it has been found hanging on walls all over the States. There is a Welsh version also, *Cariad Pur*.

There is only one difficulty in writing for Michael. He wants his lyrics at least a week before he has actually asked for them, and the asking can be at any time, after midnight or at the crack of dawn. I remember once having a very early call. He ordered in a galloping voice, words for a hymn in a five, five, five, five, five metre. Half awake I told him that I had never written in such a silly metre and that I was not in a hymnal mood in any case, as I was about to catch a bus into Cardigan. I got no consideration, just a blunt 'Write it on the bus then.'

Against normal common sense, he always gets his own way. I found a clear back of an old envelope, and, at the third attempt, found a biro that worked, before I boarded a bus. It took about fifteen minutes to get to Cardigan. Getting off, I had four verses of a simple, if not a particularly well thought-out hymn. I have told you already of my good Samaritan Jackie in the hairdressing salon, my saviour on many occasions. This time I raced to her better half, Llwyd Edwards, an excellent architect in the town. I wanted to get rid of my botched creation immediately. Llwyd and I had quite a problem deciphering my

185

illegible writing, but with huge sighs of relief, we faxed it there and then to Michael. He gave it the title 'Cenarth', either to placate me for his continuous bullying, or, to be fair, because he is a very kind-hearted man. I have been a little distressed about the unpolished simple hymn because it has been used along the years as the opening item in all the well-attended concerts that Michael, as the then conductor of *Côr Cymraeg De Califfornia*, has presented in various venues throughout California.

It was a thrill, when the choir came over in 2003, to hear them performing 'Cenarth' in the village Methodist chapel, where our own tenor, Washington James, also delighted the Californians with an appropriate aria.

Still in America

The last twenty years or so I have criss-crossed America pretty well in my haphazard way of reaching destinations. When Eira was with me, we even did Mexico. Got there in a private plane. Did everything we were warned not to do. Even got propositioned by two guides to show us the night spots, but they hadn't bargained on trying to sell such an idea to two shrewd country-bred women. Brought back with me a dragon, whose weight I cannot even dare to move, and which is now employed as a guard in the hall since my car accidents, but I still frighten people with a solemn warning that it spits fire if they put a foot out of place.

That reminds me of another private plane journey. During the Côr Meibion De Cymru trip to Toronto, a friend picked me up at Niagara Falls and took me down to Philadelphia to try to trace my ancestors. Crossing the border at Buffalo, we had to be questioned. They were very fussy. In the end I noticed the inquisitor needing my life history wore a badge that told me that his name was 'Mark Phillips'. I informed him, with grave sincerity, that since he was also a redhead, it was likely that he was one of those long-lost relations I had come all the way from Wales to be re-united with. That got rid of him! Another time, in Buffalo, the whole choir was stopped and would have been severely delayed by being interrogated individually had not the choir members lined up and sung two Welsh hymns. Had an encore, too. I've always had a feeling that music could nudge us closer to world peace . . .

I did get back to Philadelphia a year or two ago on my ancestral quest. I went straight to Wilkes Barre and found a Coal Street, an Anthracite Street and a feeling that the Welsh had stamped their images all around. The museum which could, maybe have helped, was closed so I went back to Pittsburgh and got sucked into a Jazz festival. I would like to find time to go back. If anyone who reads this and who knows anything about a Mrs. Mary A. Davies, 404, Academy Street, Wilkes Barre, PA, please, please let me know. I think she is family and I really would like time to go and find her. What is more, I am convinced that one of the reasons I never wanted to set foot in America was that my grandfather had been fatally injured in an accident at work there soon after arriving. Actually my grandfather and my gran's three brothers had gone first to Patagonia during the great exodus because, like many in Wales at that time, their independent spirit rebelled against the injustice of the time. For years in my mind, I labelled them as traitors having left the Welsh colony to go to Pennsylvania. When I eventually got to Patagonia a few years ago, I forgave them. How anyone of the first settlers could have survived the desolation that faced them is hard to understand. Even today, Porth Madryn looks like a miracle. The Welsh spirit is truly indomitable.

I have been quite a few times to the east coast also – New York, Boston, Florida and such, but that side has never captivated me like the Californian areas. I remember going to the Cherry Blossom Festival in Georgia one Spring. There had been a wild storm a week before I arrived. Not a blossom left. Went back to Wales and found a gloriously colourful panorama. Even the flea market in Georgia let me down. I found a better one in Glasgow. No, give me Manhattan Beach, California, any time before Manhattan, New York.

I find the Californians eager to accept the Welsh and our culture. I made a lot of friends along the years, through poetry readings, lyrics for Michael for his concerts, giving Celtic talks, reading poems and having discussions at the Los Angeles University. I was invited by that charismatic Welsh-speaking Irishman Professor Patrick Ford to talk to his Welsh Medieval students at UCLA. It was a slightly confounding experience since not one of the students understood the Welsh language or had any family or other contact with Wales. They were, though, highly interested in their chosen subject. I found it a worthwhile visit, and luckily so did they. I glowed with pride that our old ancient language was alive and kicking, even if I was 6,000 miles from home.

There are always so many interesting people in California. Two of my favourite friends for years have been the husband-and-wife team of Tom and Ginny Kelly in Manhattan Beach, a more than delightful couple. They met through their careers in the theatre, where both have garnered sterling reputations as actors, writers, producers and directors. Tom has made over 200 films and commercials and has been nominated for an Academy Award for a documentary film, *A space to grow* and an Emmy for a TV documentary, *The Washington Drug Test*. His most lasting contribution to the arts has been as a teacher, then a professor and eventually Dean of the College of Communication and Fine Arts at Loyola Marymount University, Los Angeles, and was the founding Dean of The School of Film and Television at the university, many of his students subsequently gaining nominations for Oscar and Emmy awards in the film and TV industry. Ginny and Tom married in 1959 and, as Ginny says, have co-produced and raised seven wonderful children who are working with great success in many fields.

Ginny is herself an accomplished actress, writer and a drama teacher in schools and colleges and has found a very satisfying outlet for her creativity, writing religious plays and musical lyrics, as well as producing and directing her liturgical dramas. She won the very prestigious Jehlinger Acting Award in the women's section at the American Academy of Dramatic Arts. The runner-up in the men's section was her friend, film star Robert Redford.

I have spent happy and stimulating hours at the Kellys' home with writers, poets, actors and like-minded interesting people from various walks of life. These are memories to be cherished for all times. I have read poems at their house, been introduced to writers and been given advice and debated all manner of cultural topics at all available times.

I have been privileged to meet so many memorable people there, not forgetting that around a few corners I have bumped into a number who have left Wales to live in this land of opportunity. A few years back, I remember flying from LA to San Francisco to give a talk at a singing festival. There I was escorted by Megan Jones Davidson, living in San Jose, but originally from Cydweli, Carmarthenshire. She can be spotted, short and stubby like me, on her visits to Wales, bursting around the National Eisteddfod field. I stayed with her for a week for she insisted on driving me all that long journey back to Los Angeles. In between I had a speaking engagement and dinner at Santa Barbara, and since I had not foreseen a stay over, I did not have an appropriate outfit to wear. There would be another good friend of mine, Myra Thomas Lawrence, living there, the epitome of fashion and she would certainly notice if I was not suitably dressed. If you are *eisteddfodwyr*, you must have seen Myra, tall and sophisticated, strolling elegantly around the Maes.

So an appropriate dress for the Santa Barbara assignation became a must. Megan and I started the hunt. There are films about the anxiety and frustration of seeking the Holy Grail but believe me, looking for a size 10 dress could have inspired an Oscar-winning epic. (I am normally a size 10, but if I stay over a month in America, it becomes a size 12. You will, I trust, keep that a secret.) Now Megan is like a dog with a juicy bone, she never gives in. We trampled in and out of every shop only to be faced generally with sizes 16 and upwards. Twice we found a 14 but not only did they make me look as if I was hiding behind a curtain for committing a misdemeanour, but the colour was redder than my once unfortunate hair. In the end we found a size 10 way out in Oxnard, Ventura, almost on the doorstep of where

I first set foot in this amazing America. There was a choice of five. I bought the five.

I had another palpitating experience not long ago in San Jose. The North American Singing Festival was held there and I had been invited to be the adjudicator of the literary section of the event. I was given a 350-dollar a night bed at a glittering hotel. I am used to the outsize effect of most things in this land of plenty, and even in other countries I have come across queen-size and king-size beds, but when I went to my room, a truly sizeable room, the bed almost dwarfed it – and my five-foot, size-10 frame! I am a *Cardi* and the extravagance of this non-essential area to lay my weary body became an instant worry. My first proposed solution was to go out on the street and grab the largest body I could find to share this continent of space with me, but fortunately I managed to whip up before my eyes the utter disgust on the face of my old Sunday school teacher, Benjamin Jones, my saintly Solomon Slow. In the end, I worked out a simple solution to my dislike of waste. For four nights, I slept in each corner of the bed, and for the last night, slept dead in the middle. A sensible solution, don't you think?

There are plenty more topsy-turvy tales to relate. And more conventional, touristy ones. I went to Las Vegas – fell in love with the dancing waters outside and worried about a middle-aged woman who sat solidly for three days and nights before an insensitive slot machine that kept on coaxing her to win. Saw my long time hero Tom Jones (Sir Tom, thankfully, by now) taking the stage at the great Memorial Hall and wowing the capacity crowd with song after song, with only an occasional sip of water throughout the night to keep our Welsh phenomenon going.

Olive, Dafydd and I went by road to the Grand Canyon, Arizona. Beautiful, awesome and thought-provoking. I would really have loved to go down to talk to the Indians, who appeared way down below us, like little specks of dirt blown into our eyes. I found a little yucca plant. It was, I gathered, in its native soil. I boasted to the others for at least half an hour that it wasn't up to the standard of the beautiful blooming yuccas I have at home. I have given up trying to understand global warming, let alone yucca plants who can thrive and bloom almost the year round in Cenarth. I don't know whether it is common sense that's lacking in humans and plants these days, or is it merely my old age.

We took Route 66 back. A very memorable journey. Dafydd is a great sharer of views, thoughts and places. He has taken me many times to my favourite Getty Museum way up in the hills. The inside is always intriguing but I am forever attracted by the external architecture. It gives tremendous satisfaction. I have a very profound suspicion that I will also experience the same magical sensation if I can fit in the time to sit and stare at our new Assembly buildings in Cardiff. Wales is really moving on.

(photo: Andrew Gilbert)

With Ron Davies, the photographer.

With Lord Parry of Neyland and Trixie in Australia, 2002.

With Dr Haydn James, former
conductor of Côr Meibion De
Cymru

A portrait of Côr Meibion De Cymru's
president, Wyn Calvin M.B.E.,
by Linda Kinsey.

With Eifion Thomas, conductor of, amongst others, Côr Meibion Llanelli.

(photo: Andrew Gilbert)

With former TV weathergirl,
Jenny Ogwen

With two great friends and characters,
Dr Glyn Rhys and Rev. Towyn Jones.

With my life-saver of a mechanic,
Alan Hopkins, in Llanon

David Fielding, the never-to-be-
forgotten instigator of these memoirs!

The Welsh chapel at Los Angeles

The Californian Welsh choir in the shadow of the magnificent
outdoor organ in San Diego

Guest speaker at a dinner in Santa Barbara.

Olive and Dafydd Evans, at my second home in Manhattan Beach.

With Rosemary Beard at the
National Eisteddfod.

With the ever-helpful Walter
in Ventura.

With Michael J. Lewis in front
of another portrait of me by
Linda Kinsey.

Dr Tom Kelly, former Dean of the
television college at Loyola
Marymount University, Los Angeles.

At the Hollywood Bowl with Olive and Eira.

Reading at the wedding of Olive and Dafydd's son, Gareth, in Bel Air.

Cutting my ninetieth birthday cake with Myra at the San Pedro feast.

Gwenno Dafydd singing one of Edith Piaf's songs
at my ninetieth birthday party.

A Detour

I should have ended these memoirs a long time ago, but I'm like the old preacher at Bryn Seion who wanted to end his sermon with the wise sayings of Solomon, but had forgotten the salient points.

I'm conscious of those readers who are, even as they read this, giving me those sidelong glances that suggest that I've lost my marbles; the kind of look that I got recently when I claimed that it takes less time to go from Aberystwyth to Edinburgh than it does to go from Aberystwyth to Cenarth. But I'll tell you what, my one-time reluctant red hair, even at ninety-plus, won't take a slight like that without fighting my corner and justifying my seemingly batty geographical claim.

Olive Evans had been staying with me at Glyn-y-Mêl but was due to go to Scotland to visit some friends, so we reserved a ticket for the train journey from Aberystwyth to Edinburgh. When I gave up driving, I had an arrangement that Monty, an Italian ex-prisoner of war, married and living in Cenarth, would drive me around. Monty and Olive were great friends. He had a heart of gold and he would take Olive and Dafydd, if he was also over, on mystery tours each time they were here. Another great friend, Susan, had offered to take Olive to Aberystwyth, and I was glad because I thought that Monty's car needed a little overhaul. But Monty said that he had had it seen to and he was taking his American friend Olive to Aberystwyth station. Monty's 'bloody hells' were tumbling out, not swear words, mind, just those automatic gap-fillers probably learnt when he was struggling to master the English language. I once had cause to tackle him about these offensive expletives. He looked bewildered and I gave up any attempts to purify his speech.

Anyway, with Monty in charge, we were Aberystwyth-bound. But before we got to Llanrhystud, the ailing car came to a full stop. No coaxing would move the stubborn body. This was a crisis. There was a train to catch. A very friendly van-driver stopped to assess our distress. He could tow us to the next lay-by, but then would have to leave us. We accepted the offer. He offered us hope, too, by saying that there was a service bus to Aberystwyth following behind. Wonderful news. All was not lost. Olive and I would go on the bus and after seeing her on the train to Edinburgh, I'd get straight back to sort out Monty and the car.

Olive caught her train, with about fifteen minutes to spare. Time to sit and talk a little. Suddenly without any warning, the train was away? and I was still on it! When the ticket collector came along, I told him bluntly that I wouldn't pay: the train had kidnapped me, after all. I was getting worried. The train might be a straight-through one to Shrewsbury and I wasn't going to risk the penalty of ringing the emergency bell. The ticket man assured me that the train would stop at the next station, Borth. I breathed again. Leaving an emotional Italian by the roadside with a crippled car was cause enough for palpitation. I had never been to Borth by train and my sense of direction was, as ever, unreliable. I had to double check which was the right platform to take me back to Aberystwyth. I was told emphatically there was only one platform. Olive and I delivered a compound sigh of relief. At Borth, I was deposited on this deserted platform which had 'the forgotten land' stamped on it. No sign of life, not even a crow for company.

The man did say there would be a train – sometime. The sometime became a very long wait. Then I cheered up. There at last was a human being coming towards me. I blinked two or three times: he was wearing a kilt. Surely I couldn't have arrived in Scotland? It was early morning and, even if I had been the alcoholic type, there was only dew around to be drunk. The man was quite chatty. Yes, a train would lumber along in its own good time. We chatted on. No good sulking: it wasn't the kilted man's fault that they had sly trains kidnapping innocent passengers in Wales. He pointed to the only building in sight – almost as far away as my tired eye could see, on the horizon. It was his brother-in-law's place. He was the Horticulturalist for Cardiganshire. Ah! My questions came faster than the pellets in a competitive hail storm.' How does your brother-in-law get rid of that indiscriminate weed, horse's tail?' He hadn't found a remedy. In fact my Scottish friend himself had, according to him, a whole continent contaminated by these bold green parasites. He said he would like to come and see my horses' tails next time he visited Wales. We were fast becoming bosom friends. I filled him in on the saga of my kidnapping, adding that if the government had left well alone instead of shabbily shunting the old GWR into the wilderness, I wouldn't be at that moment worrying that the Italian I had inconveniently left on the roadside was probably, at that very moment, having heart surgery. He looked a bit protective when he realised that a peasant like myself had been sucked into this catastrophe.

To balance matters, he told me that he was at his brother-in-law's house as his sister's son had married an American and were over here on their honeymoon. Ah! America. I was interested. Where in America did they get married? Santa Barbara. That name spelled terror. I asked him nervously to reassure me that the wedding party had not brought any snakes over with them. He looked a bit confused and then got over it and said happily 'So, you have heard of Santa Barbara.' I said 'Of course' and added that I'd been there a few times. He gave me the ultimate strange look and walked the length of the platform away from me. Eventually, he came back slowly, shaking his head as if to make sure it was still attached to his shoulders. Standing quite a distance away, he threw the next line at me: 'Do you mean to tell me that you have been to America?' Well even an elderly Welsh woman has her pride. I answered the doubting Scot: 'Of course I've been to America. I never wanted to go in the beginning but for years now I travel there on my own, two or three times a year, mostly to Los Angeles, San Diego, Santa Barbara and San Francisco.' He didn't say a lot after that but came to stand closer. I felt as if a guardian angel had dropped down from the heavens to look after me.

After what seemed like a lifetime the train came. I had actually been waiting over two-and-a-half-hours. I had given up on Monty, hoping that he had found somebody to get the car going again. My very caring Scot, I concluded, had worked out that I was in my second childhood and as a Good Samaritan helped me into the train, and caringly sat besides me. When we got to Aberystwyth, I aimed to find the first bus that would take me back to a disconsolate and emotional Italian. My Scot even saw that my foot was safely on the bus step before he left, letting out, I think, a huge sigh of relief. Did he think I was a nutcase? I think it was probably Dafydd who later explained to me the poor kilted man's confusion; after all, a ridiculously old woman who travelled on her own, two or three times a year, to California, and then allowed herself to be kidnapped by a train in rural Wales, must be considered at least a near-psychiatric case.

My problems were not yet over. When I entered the fairly crowded bus, I could hear whisperings. Little phrases hit me like 'Yes it's her. I saw her recently on TV.' You could feel sly glances. I stood speechless before the driver, totally embarrassed. Where did I want to go? I didn't have a clue. The crowd of people wishing me to declare my destination would, like my kilted friend, think I was afflicted mentally. I asked the driver timidly if he had seen a broken-down car in a lay-by somewhere between Llanon and Llanrhystud. No, he hadn't noticed one. Maybe Monty had found someone to repair it and gone home. I had been gone for hours. He must have been bored waiting. I became more embarrassed. I had to settle on getting a ticket to somewhere. Then my grey cells started to react. I had paid the driver who picked Olive and me up at the lay-by, for two single 90p tickets. The driver, who had a kind face, looked happily relieved. In a voice that the whole bus could hear, he told me 'I know exactly which lay-by to take you to.' Apparently, Monty had been blocking each bus heading for Cardigan, and had been insisting on entering each one to make sure I wasn't on it and trying to ignore the poor helpless car. I knew the driver had the warmth of a Cardiganshire heart for he ordered me to sit in the bus and he assured me that he and Monty would have a look under the bonnet of the car. That man had the makings of a saint. And fair play, the passengers should also be recommended. By now they were openly gossiping with me and not one murmur against this extravagant delay in getting to their homes.

Monty and the bus driver had their heads under the bonnet for what must have been over twenty minutes (the similarity to two ostriches did occur to me but luckily I kept mum). Their final diagnosis – the coil had gone and the car needed to be fitted with a new one. I said a very large and sincere thank you to the driver and asked him if he could drop us at the Llanrhystud garage as I knew the owners. No. He had other plans. He was taking us to Llanon, where he lived and where a new garage had opened. He knew they would see to fitting in a new coil. He delivered us there and came across himself to make sure that the young mechanic in charge had the right instructions.

Whilst he was fixing the coil, the young mechanic's mother came to talk to me. They had just opened this garage and left her husband running another garage somewhere across the country. She would be all alone when the son went to fix the coil, so would I consider staying with her to look after the office if people called for petrol? After all the kindnesses shown that day, I willingly agreed. And did I feel proud? This was the first offer of a job, apart from my war service in police courts, I had ever had.

When Monty and I got back finally to Glyn-y-Mêl, the telephone was almost pleading to be answered. It was our friend

Olive from Edinburgh. She had been trying before and thought we were teasing when we said we had just arrived home. It was totally unbelievable that she had taken hours less time to get to Edinburgh than it took us to arrive back at Cenarth from Aberystwyth. Now you unbelievers, I am sure after hearing all my complications that you will stand by the authenticity of these memoirs.

Nearing the End and Ninety

It was a great shock when I was told in America that I would be 90 in October 2004.

I had made birthdays redundant a long time ago when we had forgotten to send birthday cards to our nephew, Stephen. At the last minute, I went out and picked some lovely ones, each with the number '5' displayed on them. My enthusiasm backfired once again. When the young toddler opened them, he found that we had gone back in time: the '5' should actually have been '7'. Such was my embarrassment that I determined to cancel all family birthdays, including my own. I would continue to honour Christmas and St David, but no more birthday cards.

Thus it was that the Los Angeles birthday celebrations were such a shock. But for a topsy-turvy little old antique, what a glorious pinnacle! I even forgot the sneaky gout and basked instead in the royal aura of King Henry VIII. Of course, like many things in my life it nearly didn't happen.

In 2003 I was over in LA as usual and pestered by Michael J. Lewis to promise that I would be there in October 2004. I almost had to sign a declaration. It came to a point when I didn't know whether Michael was trying to make out that I was senile, or that the genius himself was getting to that state much too soon. Which ever way, I wanted nothing to do with it. I would give that October a miss. I arranged to go to Alaska. Then someone let a big ginger cat out of the bag. My American friends discovered that I shared a birthday with Dylan Thomas. So, not only were they arranging a momentous celebration for my birthday but Michael J. Lewis was composing music for four of my works and four of Dylan Thomas's pieces. The excitement was infectious.

There was only one place to congregate for my ninetieth birthday celebrations – 408, 20th Street, Manhattan Beach, California. It has been my second home for almost twenty years, and I have long suspected that almost everyone who has visited California has, at one time or another, walked in through its open doors.

Further proof of this came when Dafydd was staying with me at Glyn-y-Mêl recently. A presentable gentleman called at my home, hoping, I think, to sell me an adjustable bed, having probably been alerted by some hospital to my car crashes. He realised that there would be no sale here, so we got chatting about other things. He was from Swansea, I learnt, and I introduced him to Dafydd, who thought he reminded him of someone he knew but couldn't quite place him. James Ratcliff stared back at Dafydd, and as we were discussing Manhattan, New York and Manhattan Beach, California, suddenly James told Dafydd: 'I can describe your house. At the front door there is a sun bed inside with toy bears on.' I thought the man was psychic. James, it seems, had found their open door over twenty years ago when travelling on his way to Chicago and had been invited to stay.

Dafydd has a nose for getting acquainted with and helping everyone. I was standing with him outside the new LA Music Centre a year or so ago. Dafydd picked out a Welsh accent and went across to talk to the man and his family. They were touring around and came from Bridgend, like Dafydd. It turned out that the man's mother and Dafydd's mother had lived next door to each other just outside Nantymoel. Oh, yes. 408, 20th Street is well known to very many people.

I still feel ashamed, however, that America had to alert me to my birthday, especially my ninetieth one. Everyone was so supportive. I even felt sorry that Dylan Thomas wasn't there to celebrate with us. I had the whole Californian Welsh choir rooting for me and heaps of other friends. I had VIP treatment from the word 'Go' at Heathrow. I have since worked out that it was the well-known Euryn Ogwen and his lovely wife, Jenny, who had arranged my royal treatment there. They are always so helpful. We have been friends for years. I do miss Jenny forecasting the weather. Even when she forecast rain, her Pembrokeshire voice and cheerful outlook would every time save me, and very many others, from bouts of depression.

I encountered another touch of Pembrokeshire magic when the film crew commissioned by S4C to cover the event gathered into the Evanses' home. Their producer was Euros Wyn, a delightful young man. I had interviewed his father many moons ago, when he was a senior student at Ysgol y Preseli, the comprehensive school in Crymych. He, like his son, was charming and easy to work with. I can still remember it – it was my first ever interview. My sincere thanks to Euros for his care of his elderly topsy-turvy victim. He even arranged to carry home to Wales my weighty birthday presents.

There was yet another added Pembrokeshire presence, too: Gwenno Dafydd. We met about 18 years ago when she telephoned to ask if she could come and pick my brains, as she was writing a one-woman show about my friend Edith Piaf. We both realised we shared a passion for Piaf, Pwllderi, creative writing and adventures, and have been firm friends ever since. Gwenno was nurtured by mystic Pencaer where Dewi Emrys roamed as a child and was also involved in interviewing with the TV crew. She has always been a great singer of Piaf songs and had volunteered to sing at my birthday feast. I confess that her 'La vie en rose' and 'Je ne regrette rien' brought tears to many eyes on that emotional night.

Rhodri, the cameraman, was quite a surprise. He had an uncanny eye for focusing on unusual objects. My great niece's father-in-law is an American, and lives now not far from me. He was delighted with the TV transmission when he saw me being interviewed sitting flat on my behind with miles of sand around me. He recognised the beach as the one used in the *Baywatch* TV series! I have sat there many times but I must admit being a

201

bit disgruntled when people keep on asking me 'Who helped you up?' I may be old but I assure that I will not let go of my genuine friend, independence, until I absolutely must.

The young crew did a grand job. There was, amazingly enough, only one near hiccup. Rhodri wanted to film me going the whole length of the regally beautiful Palos Verdes in an open-top limousine. I had taken time in the morning to have a special hairdo in case I came face to face with my elegant friend, Myra, and if I looked a mess she would think I was letting Wales down. It was a lovely day but with a breeze brisker than the one at Borth above Aberystwyth, surely the windiest place on earth. My hairdo was totally ruined. On the journey back the wind became egotistic. The best way to deal with an immovable object is to ignore it. I concentrated on my open royal carriage and decided to mimic the late Queen Mother's personal affectionate wave. By the end of the journey, I had perfected it. Myra from Santa Barbara would have been delighted. I forgot the wispy, undignified mess covering my harrowed scalp. All in all, it was an honourable start to proceedings.

There were three glorious birthday concerts. Michael J. Lewis, if anything, surpassed himself. He had chosen to set Dylan Thomas's 'Dear Gwalia', 'Come and sweep my Chimbley', 'The Reverend Eli Jenkins's Sunset poem' and 'Do not go Gentle into that Good Night'. A great tribute. Michael's choice of my poems were 'Cenarth'; 'Myra (God of Love)' in appreciation of Myra Thomas Lawrence's years of tutoring the ethnic choir to pronounce the Welsh words in the perfect language of heaven; 'True Love' and 'La Môme Piaf'. In between, no one at the concerts can ever forget the sounds of those perennially uplifting Welsh hymns, 'Cwm Rhondda' and 'Aberystwyth', sung by the choir, the audiences and every other soul within hearing distance of what my American friends called ' A Celebration of Welsh Poets'. I really was sad that my birthmate, Dylan, was not with us to enjoy the celebrations. We had such a truly outsize American welcome. The wonder of being ninety years old at these celebrations was awesome and absolutely captivating. The love and affection surrounding me 6,000 miles from home was beyond the realm of dreams.

Our first concert was at Saint Paul's Cathedral, San Diego, and the second at the Presbyterian Chapel, Wiltshire Street, Los Angeles, where we had the added blessing of the biggest organ in the world. I remember standing there mesmerised, trying to imagine my little Bryn Seion chapel at home fitted into a tiny corner of this vast arena. I could see John the Blower, eyes tightly shut, pumping energy into what we thought was our highly fashionable organ. We went all the way to San Francisco for the third celebratory concert. There I was richly honoured to have my work sung at the remarkable Grace Cathedral. The entrance door itself of intricate gold designs was beyond thought. I felt proud and privileged.

This celebrating was contagious. After the concert, a few of us were invited to another special party at Myra's apartment in San Francisco. What a top up! I guess you must all think that after struggling along ninety miles of life, the sensible order would be for a little beauty sleep. I do probably look now like the grotesque half of Picasso's 'Ugly Woman', but then why should I care when I can boast that that was how the great man Picasso himself would have portrayed me.

And what of the bash at The Whale and Ale, the British Pub in San Pedro? There is always a great welcome there from the owner, Andrew Silber. The whole choir was there at the ready, my friends from far and near, the locals and every stray passer-by had been drawn into this celebration. The goodies, the huge birthday cake, the presents and the drinks for the thirsty and non-thirsty were all liberal and mountainous. Dylan would have loved it.

Life after Ninety

I have travelled by road from San Francisco to Los Angeles a number of times. If you do sometime, take a break at a place called Cambria. I would love to tell you exactly where it is, but with no sense of direction, I can only assure you that it is located somewhere between those two busy cities. In any case, in these days of Navigation Satellites, just whisper where you want to go, and the car will take you there. Prayer must be my weakest link, for how many times did I sit at the wheel of my car praying that it would take me to my destination? – but it never did. Now my friends are gloating over their new gadget. And most of them were born with a sense of direction.

The resort of Cambria is a mini Wales. A Welsh-American, from Pennsylvania, saw the place, found it resembled the old country and named it Cambria. The moment I first saw it, I felt strangely at home as if in Llangrannog, in my native Cardiganshire, or any of the other small resorts dotted along the Welsh coastline. Dafydd and Olive took me there and I was so impressed with the likeness between Wales and Cambria that I wrote a little 'thank you' there and then:

Sound of the Sea.

When I came to Cambria, I came to my Wales,
its sun with warm kisses, its boisterous gales.
    The whiteness of welcome in the dancing foam
filled my heart with contentment in this home from home.
    And the Host and Hostess in this delightful setting
set my ninety years at peace with their tender caring.

Dafydd was, as ever, a first-class guide. He showed me all the exciting places. I had never before seen a group of elephant seals on the sea shore, knitted together like a ribbed Scottish Island counterpane, and half asleep waiting for the males to come ashore to mate. We did the Highway Run, too and the famous Dig Sur. If the film crew had had more time when over for the celebration, I would have liked Wales to have seen a few shots of its lookalike, Cambria. Over the years I find that the world is getting ridiculously intimate. Years ago when I was mostly a lone traveller, I did not expect to find Welsh connections around every corner. Although I must admit that even long ago the Welsh have never been backward in coming forward, as my old friend Dafi Jams, Bwlchmelyn (he who saved my life) would always remind us.

After the original warm and giggling welcome to the USA by the two 'strange' ladies, I found out that Olive was originally from London, whilst her friend Gill had Welsh connections. Her family came from around Cardigan and Newcastle Emlyn, almost perched on my doorstep. In fact, I knew her cousins well. They owned a busy garage in the town and I had been buying petrol there for years. They are retired now, but I still see them occasionally and invariably they shout at me 'Have you just come back again. How were they over there this time'? It's so gratifying to forget those thousands of miles between us. Wouldn't it be wonderful if we were all friendly around the world and wished each other well?

Gill and Olive are the two loveliest ladies in America. But since, at last, I'm trying to straighten out the bends of this lengthy road of life, I think it is time to confess that for years I have been quite envious of Gill. She has an instinct for buying high-class goods, and with subtle manoeuvres can turn bargaining into a fine art. I don't think I am naturally an envious person and I am not proud that I spent years yearning to match Gill's excellence. My mother would have given me a strict telling-off, but my gran would have said with a sly wink, 'Go for it girl, and learn from the expert.'

The unthinkable can happen even at ninety years and more: I have, at last, bought an article at half price! A real bargain and all on my own. Gill might disapprove of my method and I did argue with myself whether I would keep this dubious side of my character secret. In the end I had to admit that, in spite of my disapproval of egotists, it turns out that I am one of them. The truth is, after infiltrating my longish memory and exposing all my mishaps to the world, I didn't want you all to write me off as a complete loser. When you reach your ninetieth birthday, everybody insists you can say anything you like. I hope that can be extended to doing anything you like also, and if you find my method surreal, please can you still join in my happiness? I am so proud of this one unexpected success.

I think it's only fair to try to explain how it all happened. I think you will realise as I did, that there was a kind of sacred aura over the whole adventure. It all started with an invitation from my long-time friend, the Rev. Towyn Jones, Carmarthen. He was president of the centenary celebrations of the Carmarthenshire's Antiquarian Society at the Bishop's Palace, Abergwili, near Carmarthen, in 2006. There would be other friends there and we would all be dressed in Edwardian finery. He mentioned the date. I found I would be back home a day or two before the event. I was more than happy until he mentioned that the ladies were expected to wear hats. It's all very disconcerting considering all my fights over my provoking red hair, but I have never, ever been a wearer of hats. The only time I disciplined myself to wear one was at the wedding of Dafydd and Olive's son, Gareth. I had been invited to read a poem I had written at the wedding ceremony held at the chapel at Bel Air, where the ex-President Ronald Reagan was a member. There were to be 550 guests in this golden area of California. I guess you would agree that a hat there was a must. But anywhere else, never.

The Rev. Towyn can be very persuasive. Fair play, Towyn will help anybody. I felt a bit mean, but the thought of wearing a hat fought a tigerish battle with my accident-prone brain. In the end it was the shadow of fear that made me accept, hat and all. Towyn has an expert knowledge of ghosts, after all. What if I were black-listed by my refusal to help? I again heard my grandmother's voice – 'Don't ever argue with anybody who has an intimate knowledge of ghosts'.

I had only three days to get myself into Edwardian gear. You know now how useless a topsy-turvy person is at organising. I hurried down to Jackie, my ever knowledgeable hairdresser. Where would I find somewhere where I could hire an Edwardian outfit? She gave me several telephone numbers. I began to feel better.

I was walking up High Street, Cardigan, pondering profound thoughts, when I came to a dreamlike stop. The smart Morris clothes shop I knew well was changing hands. Half the window was being assembled with all kinds of shop models dressed in period costumes. I didn't stop to think. As ever, I marched in. Could they find me an Edwardian outfit? The two assistants were very willing to help in the middle of their very important first window display. We pored over a catalogue. You know my handicap? Even if I had wanted to join the police in the old days, they wouldn't have had me, I was way too short. Even that has changed: they seem to accept them now baby-faced from primary schools.

All the outfits on show were long tunics. I only had tomorrow to reshape anything. I found one that looked as if it had a top and skirt. The assistant said it had, and I could order it for the following day. I went for it. £30 for hiring for two days. Things were looking up. One problem, however: I have no sewing sense. But redheads can be stubborn in emergencies. I worked out that I could shorten the skirt at the waist and my awkward stitches could be hidden under the top. I went home feeling proud of my entrepreneurship.

I was at the shop in good time next day. But in my life, nightmares can become instant daymares: the top and bottom of the suit were not separate. There was no way I could shorten it without damage. In the end, worn down by my tearful pleading and distress, and my genuine fear of ghostly reprisals, the assistants had an emergency confrontation and agreed to sell me the outfit for £30, the hiring fee. Luckily there was no time to prevaricate. I double-backed home, cut the top from the bottom, made a hem at the waist with elephant stitches, and found some knicker elastic to push through the seam. I had an elegant skirt down to my toes.

Then my next problem. There were white ruffles around the sleeves, so how could I find a blouse to match? I had recently exchanged my caravan and had washed the old net curtains. Ideal. I ironed a long length, made a hole in the centre for my head, sewed a seam round the neck and two holes for my arms, then sneaked some more elastic, coaxed it into the seam, and *voila*, I had a ruffled collar. I convinced myself I was a stylish Edwardian. I hunted round and found some white gloves from some wedding or other, and, I'm convinced, with non-terrestial help, that I was guided to find, hiding behind a bardic chair in the hall, an umbrella plastered with passion flowers that I had brought back all the way from Mexico. It became a delightful parasol. I had a perfectly decent black shawl but couldn't find it. I telephoned Rosemary, a good and always helpful friend whom I had first met out in California, but who had retired and was now living in Ammanford. She had rather a nice German shawl, and hearing of my emergency, gave an assurance that she would go there and then to post it to arrive in time for this auspicious event.

Life was almost at the feelgood stage but for that elusive hat. I really had tried fitting one or two, but each one looked as if I was wearing a coracle to go on a poaching spree and what would any decent ghost think of that? An excuse for murder more than likely.

I thought of sending Towyn an email to explain. But wouldn't that be cowardly and insulting? And what about my gran's advice: 'If you're ever cornered, stand your ground'? No.

There was only one way out. I would go to Carmarthen to face the disappointed holy gentleman.

With a depressed face and lagging feet, I was walking up Lammas Street aiming for the Reverend's residence. Halfway up the street on your right, there's a cute little shop. If you know Carmarthen, you'll know it. Its window always has a display of unusual clothes. Never hats, though. I am not a window shopper, but this window draws me like a magnet. My dentist lives off Lammas Street so I have stared many, many times at it. This time, in spite of my worries, I couldn't resist a quick peep. I came to an abrupt halt. I had an eerie feeling. Surely the ghosts wouldn't be that vindictive, showing a hat in the corner, where there had never been a hat before? I looked down at my feet. They were solidly on the ground. I pushed my spectacles back on my nose. I think because of the structure of my nose, mine have a habit of sitting on the tip and distorting my sight. No, the hat was still there. It looked as light as the mature head of a dandelion, one whiff of wind and it would be wafted to oblivion. I didn't hesitate any longer and ran into the shop. Another customer had snatched the hat and was holding it. There were two cheerful assistants in attendance. I actually delivered a prayer aloud to make certain it could be heard. It worked. The hat was handed back. Seeing my obsessive tactics, the hat was placed on my head. It didn't even bruise my brain. This hat was definitely mine. One of the assistants whispered 'Have you seen the price?' I thought it was a silly question but to show I was streetwise, even though I was so old, I looked at the price tag. I looked again, and a third time. Ninety nine pounds, ninety nine pence (the 99p always infuriates me.) All that money for a hat for just one day. Common sense seeped back. I had been a *Cardi* for most of my life. Reluctantly I handed back this lightweight temptation. I'm sure the assistants gave a sigh of relief. I jumped on the first bus for home.

The bus journey was not my usual fun ride. In fact it was an uncomfortable battle with my conscience for all of the one hour and thirty minutes. My battered brain was working overtime. How could I find a way of buying that hat and not feel guilty? I was in a no-win situation.

As I wearily unlocked the door of my little pink bungalow, there was a sudden flash of inspiration. I made straight for the telephone in the hall. I called my niece Annie. I was lucky. She answered in person. I explained about the expensive hat and slightly embroidered a little in the telling of my inspiring solution. Annie has a quick grasp of emergency situations. Yes, she and her friends were still into theatricals, and so was her daughter Rachel, a speech writer in Parliament. There would be no problem in hiring out the hat. It would probably be profit-making. I didn't waste any time on family gossip.

I got the first bus to Carmarthen at an unearthly hour the following morning and I was standing eagerly at the shop door. When it opened a tiny crack, I pushed myself in. Yes, my hat with ostrich feathers intact, was still there. I took it firmly in my hand but consciences can be so predictably unpredictable. I suddenly thought of my friend Gill and how she had worked so hard to instil in me the sense of joy in manoeuvring a bargain. I am not averse to bettering myself by whatever means. Maybe this was my one and only chance.

The two cheery assistants of the day before had been replaced by a rather solemn-looking but nice enough young lady. I elaborated my idea in as simple a way as I could in order to get a favourable response. I stood before the serious assistant in what I assumed was a bargain theatrical pose and explained my reasonable request.

If I went out now and robbed the nearest bank and got the necessary one hundred pounds, less one penny, to pay cash for the hat, would I get a reduction in the price? I got a very sullen stare as she backed away. The silence became uncomfortable and I had to admit to her that perhaps it was not a good proposition after all.

But surely a *Cardi* on the scent of a bargain should never

give up. I tried another line of reasoning. I stressed the fact that I was 91 plus years of age, and surely Carmarthen, county next door to Ceredigion, should give a sizeable reduction to such an ancient customer? After another long stare, the assistant muttered something about telephoning. My mind came back to the awesome ghosts? Would the police come in exaggerated force to lock me up for trying to get money by false pretences? If they X-rayed me for security, would my black conscience work for me or against me? In the split instant that I decided to put the hat down where it would not be blown away, and run before I was handcuffed, the assistant came back. The smile across her face had more warmth than the South African sun that once caressed my face. Her voice was pure melody as she said 'The owner says you can have the hat for £50.' In my startled excitement, I thanked her in Welsh, English and even French, which I thought I had scrubbed out of my life for ever.

My first bargain. A 50% reduction! Actually half price! Gill would be so proud of me. I don't think I will tell her in detail how I managed it. I also vowed silently that I would never again utter one disparaging word against the Rev. Towyn's ghosts.

Of course, the reality is, even with all my ego-boasting, I came nowhere near Gill's standard. She owns beautiful artistic treasures and two houses in California. But my gran's voice did tell me 'Go for it girl'. And I did give it my best shot.

There is just one more confession I would like to unload on you. Another, I suppose, of the many temptations I failed to resist.

I was walking along the Bay in Cardiff when the construction workers were laying the foundation of the Millennium Centre. The concrete was enticingly wet. Would it be an unforgivable sin? My eyes slithered slyly everywhere. It was lunch time. No visible workers. I forced my back to bend under the protective wire and put my foot boldly as far in as I could reach. My footprint in concrete in the Millennium wonder! I have a feeling that my gran would have approved.

Signing Off

As a topsy-turvy person, I have inevitably been ordered throughout my life to do – and not to do – things. Sometimes I agreed. Sometimes I didn't! It was very, very reluctantly that I agreed to travel these miles of reminiscences. There is another recurring request, however, that I am happier to agree, namely for an English translation of my Falklands poem, *Clymau* ('Bonds'). Having got these memoirs out of the way, I have decided to obey and deliver.

BONDS. KNOTS. TIES.

1865
Through the mist, sounds of moving at Pant Glas
and a woman's wailing;
the muteness of remembering;
a locked gate a final sting.

A voiceless yard groans noisily; in the barn
mice squeaking merrily;
an anchorless family
pushed rudderless out to sea.

An oppressive squirearchy
breaks up a home without mercy;
the orphaned furniture
dragged on a dray along a lane of mud.

A pot-bellied dictator geared into power
by plebeian robots;

a pompous traitor
preening himself in the cuckoo's nest.

The dispossessed, a man of God, honouring
his acres of heritage;
willing for his generation, freedom of thought
without the shadow of fear.

The Court Bailiff took up duties; stock and implements
shied under the hammer.
The day, a day of burial.
Work ceased, The joy of living ended.

*   *   *

Venturing into Liverpool, as yet
a mystic name in the mother tongue;
whirlwinds of emotion churning into currents,
flooding their souls with nightmares of horror.
Ties of family tighten, the love of Pant Glas
binding them in its tendrils of grief.

Slowly, slowly moved the Mimosa
towards the heaven of Patagonia.
A voyage of vomit and plague.

Shaking off the dust of oppression,
an awakened conscience eyeing on a fair horizon
a land of plenty, and the pride of freedom
to restart a new life of hope.

Ailing centuries of sailing,
the anguish of *hiraeth* like the tear of a claw;
gallantly singing in the presence of the English
who had no cause to suffer their indignity of heart.

Children, trampling the boards of adventure,
wildly uncaring in an uneasy storm,
not yet having recognised pain.

Losing a daughter in their adversity,
abandoning the golden tresses to the wastes of ocean,
and the sea closing around her.

He, who defied the law,
humbly on his knees, eyes full of dried tears,
his remaining family his only hope.

A broken-hearted mother bending beneath her burden,
craving with emotion,
an answer to the age-old question.

They blamed the oppressive law; they bow to Fate.
They lose a daughter in spite of prayer;
one who was flesh of their flesh.

Through trials of despair and covering of weals,
there comes a peace
an ecstasy of hope in the sighting of land,
and a journey's end.

Taking leave of the mountains of ocean;
of a cabin that was an altar;
of a daughter cradled at the bottom of the sea.

The heart is knotted in grief
for the fairness amid the sea-weed.
Losing her was losing the sight of one's eye.

*   *   *

A never-ending July throws a snowy welcome;
Mimosa dances on the ocean edge.
Parcels of dishearted flesh unloaded their dreams
once more ground into dust.

Headland thrusting their jowls into a bleak sea
at the end of the bay;
dried out skeletons
like the remains of wizened old dragons.

A tight knot of *hiraeth*
strangles their heroism.
And the waves laugh on the sea shore.

*   *   *

An exile, folding his family like a blanket around him,
hurls his mattocks at the root of a sturdy thorn;
raping unceasingly the virginity of desert, his eyes
reflecting the garden of Eve.

Churning in a wilderness, his pickaxe
bouncing uncaringly off the face of parched earth;
aching for a patch of the green grass of tomorrows,
and the day an eternity of nothingness.

Exploring daily through diligent hours,
like the legend Arthur seeking the Holy Grail.
And a day of wonder. A crystal stream gushing
out of the vessel of desolation.

Building a house; planning a home. A second Pant Glas
out of the mountainous ashes of nightmares;
a shelter from the storm of uprooting;
a crude structure. A seventh heaven.

Weary of work, their spirits uplifted by the rousing hymns
of a Bethel reborn.
And the God of Wales, God of the prairie.

*   *   *

1982
Briars have spun a death-wish over the Mansion;
rats are at-home in its cowsheds and stables;
co-bedding hippies carpeting floors, and the Squire's cellar,
without lock, a lair for the homeless.

Privileged rich swarm the Fair Valley sucking
the nectar of summer homes;
Rudely ravishing local ties of togetherness, a pleasure boat
grinning in the old cart-house.

The Mill has become a retreat
for the super-annuated childless;
sold for a fat £40,000.

There is no one left at the Chapel House, no one
but a red-lipped foreigner
and a nanny goat worshipping at the door.

Tombstones groan between earth-nut flowers;
the churchyard gate wide open
like the mouth of the mindless forever gaping.

A yew tree weeps
over the remains of old characters.
The lies of the grave cannot be undone.

*   *   *

The son of Pant Glas is on the Brecon Beacons, a young lad
clad in Khaki, his toy gun grown real;
lured by promises of joy times roving the world,
his wallet bulging.
Abandoning the plough and harrow to a rusty death,
to take up shooting and stabbing with bayonet.

Turning his back on a pregnant dole-queue, his horizon
undimmed by the shadow of war.
Could one ever wish for a better choice?

Grovelling through coarse growth,
screaming madly across green grass
to stab men of straw.

A General, golden leeks, cap and tunic, poring
over detail sketch-maps, sending troops
to pin-pricked swamps.

Lips of red roses
and dirt black faces
attack, wave after wave.

Feeling, without seeing, in the light of day, eyes
staring from enemy terrain;
when the sun falls asleep, night glasses gaze back
like the two querying eyes of an ox.

A soldier clad in a fair weather suit, as yet
not accepting the technique of killing.

Through tedious hours of hell, he sees
with closed eyes, his paradise Pant Glas;
the face of his sweetheart in a crystal clear pool,
and he locks the image of love in his heart.

A kiss of sunshine peeping through leaves, encircling a finger
of a gorse bush with a golden band;
sipping the virtue of ripe blackberry wine;
the moon's ballet a smile on the smoothness of lake.

The harsh bark of the sergeant-major
shatters the ties of romantic dreams
to lie buried in the churchyard of memory.

There comes a payday at the end of the week,
and the riotous joy of a night to remember.
War will not enter his domain.
Pant Glas shall forever be free of pain.

A short respite of hope; a retreat from duty,
with his passionate girl from Cae Meillion farm;
and the blackthorn needles busily sewing
a fence of love enclosing two hearts.

Drowning the sorrows of a grizzly life;
wrapping peace in a cloak of fur;
peering at Spring calling a tree to life;
carving a memory in the bark of an oak.

Like a clap of thunder, the call to rejoin.
Bidding farewell to hopes and desires, he spies
at the corner of the field of gorse; a ewe
in the seething pangs of birth.

Sir Galahad, beast of prey, is waiting, mouth ajar
like the jaws of a whale;
tanks sinking dutifully into her belly;
hoary guns
bristling on the nape of her neck.
The warring pride of her ilk on the ocean
as she thrusts anchor before the storm.

The son of Pant Glas at the centre of conflict, henceforth
an atom in the ship's manifest.
A machine to kill, a robot on a voyage of doom
across acres of water.
A lad at the Spring of life, his gun night and day
his close, lonely companion.

*   *   *

When the waves snarl into a temper, he recalls
the saga of the adventure to Patagonia, and the sighting
of land after aeons of time
in the entrails of the Mimosa.

He, voyaging in the same direction, his passage paid
from the nation's purse.
In his heart there glows the same desire of reaching land,
his training geared to another conquest.
He sees endless seas stretching to far horizons, and a whale,
a lookalike of the beast in the Book of Revelation.

A chill falls, like icicles on a day of battle,
in spite of bonds that tie Patagonia and the homeland of Wales;
two small countries under a cloud, their anguish
an unbearable burden to hold.

Fear of seeing a battleship on the horizon;
fear of a fatal weapon darting its snare;
fear of a submarine creeping lowly;
fear of a bomb born to explode.
Fear of the silent calm in its aching monotony; and fear
of a grave forever between the coral.

There will be no tears or gilded memorials
above the bones on 'No Man's Seas'.

*   *   *

Buenos Aires in cloud and sunshine resounds
to the tramp of celtic feet;
proud descendants of the old heroic who fled
the oppression of a land of love.
We have met in reunion on the Thursdays of Hiraeth –
kindred rejoicing in our Festival of Hope.

The City of adoption a bubble of passion;
the Casa Rosada a hive full of dance;
years on through dispute and blinkered obstructions
the Malvinas are surely theirs to hold.

Dawns a day of Armageddon;
darkness over the whiteness of waves.
A day of black sun; of clawing of breasts.

A Mirage swoops,
dropping death from its clutches,
before fleeing home over rocky banks.

Sir Galahad is a ball of fire;
bundles of khaki writhe in water
to escape the lips of a hellish flame.

Wasps of helicopters
sucking the breathing into their bellies
before the closing of the eyes of hope.

A cruel death to their tomorrows
in the Valhalla of scorching pain.
From their heroism they will not return.

The truth is born on a day of insanity; false values
are decrutched and fall by the way.

Britain and Argentina, homes of compatriots, are carrying
the indelible mark of Cain.

Burying the dead who will see no Summer on a June day
in a winter of discontent;
carting the wounded willy-nilly
to a freezer shed, once for animal flesh.
Urging the near-dying to an impromptu ward and the lads
sons, husbands, sweethearts, and dutiful enemies,
co-suffering under a roof with a Cross.

From the mouth of a bottle, a Britisher's blood
flows slowly into an Argentinian arm;
warm blood of men, lovers of homeland,
mingling in harmony in each other's veins.

*   *   *

Who is he who sees but blackness
in a hospital ward in the shed in San Carlos?
A lad whose every day is now a one night.

He listens to the sounds of the busyness of living,
staring emptily without seeing, fingering
the vastness of his calamity.

Eyeless sockets gaping,
gaping unceasingly
into the long night of groan.

When morphia eases the weals of wounds,
he again walks tall on endearing paths,
across the pastures from Pant Glas to Cae Meillion,
and a winsome maiden leaps into his arms.

He sees the carving of love in the bark of an oak;
a cluster of blood-buds on a mountain ash;
Jesus of Bethel hanging on a nearby bush, and Death
lurking in the shadow of an old yew tree.

With sightless eyes he sees a meadow thrilling with lambs,
and the face of a mother whom he will see no more.

But who is this approaching his tortuous bed?
A youth from Buenos Aires in battle.

A kindred of the peasant poor
who fled the City one harsh winter
from the reality of Cwm Hyfryd.

Years on, a legacy remains on lip;
little words of mystic virtue
urging themselves into unmanageable slots.

The one-armed greeting the blind.
And a bond is forged
despite two nations in conflict.

Celts, with warm blood of belonging coursing through veins;
sharing the legacy of an ancient tongue;
two souls apart, yet of common heritage.

The bonds are stronger than the wounds.
Is there a hope of bridging the gap?

Raggedly fitful the communication.
Then, sadly, separation.

Is a black future the only forever?

Nothing remains but the scars of remembrance,
and the Biblical mite of a country to its glorious brave.
Endless days of fingering the letterings
of the carving of memory
in the bark of the oak tree of hope.
A lock seals the door of Cae Meillion.

What is a maid but the figment of passion
and the arrow that stabs through the heart?

The definitive fragile bond
for a son deprived of a Summer.

Acknowledgements

In thanking all my readers, those who fell by the way, and those who laughed at me, or with me, to the end, I have a few special debts of gratitude to pay.

I cannot, of course, hope to thank all my friends who urged me to commit these memoirs to paper. The subsequent birth was, admittedly, problematic. A Caesarian delivery indeed! Better I thank, therefore, those who helped me keep my initial three-week draft alive!

For the conceiving, I have long ago forgiven David Fielding and gained a trusted friend.

For saving the draft, editing it and urging its publication, I am grateful to Olive Evans, one well used to drawing her expert editorial toothcomb through the work of seasoned authors.

For the photograph that appears in the frame on the cover of the book, I thank that remarkable scientist, Dr Tegwyn Harris of Exeter. It was also his sense of humour and wisdom that kept the original draft from the rubbish bin.

My generous thanks, naturally, to Gomer Press and Ceri Wyn Jones. Once he'd understood why the work had been written in English, not in Welsh, he was a great help. I have a lot of respect for Gomer. It was they who published my first book back in 1936, and, who knows, maybe my last one now in 2007.

As a topsy-turvy person, I hope for forgiveness. What is more, I urge all the redheaded readers out there, stay true to yourselves and remember that the magic of tinting is gloriously acceptable. Today, you will even find men with rainbow-coloured hair sitting next to you on the bus!

It has been a lot of fun, and I would like to leave you with one final entreaty: try to make as many footprints in the concrete as you can – and treasure them.